AMERICAN ★ HISTORY

PROTESTS AND RIOTS

That Changed America

By Joan Stoltman

Portions of this book originally appeared in
Protests and Riots by Michael V. Uschan.

LUCENT
PRESS

Published in 2019 by
Lucent Press, an Imprint of Greenhaven Publishing, LLC
353 3rd Avenue
Suite 255
New York, NY 10010

Designer: Deanna Paternostro
Editor: Jessica Moore

Library of Congress Cataloging-in-Publication Data

Names: Stoltman, Joan, author.
Title: Protests and riots that changed America / Joan Stoltman.
Description: New York : Lucent Press, [2019] | Series: American history |
  Includes bibliographical references and index.
Identifiers: LCCN 2017057875| ISBN 9781534564152 (library bound book) | ISBN
  9781534564176 (pbk. book) | ISBN 9781534564169 (ebook)
Subjects: LCSH: Protest movements--United States--History--Juvenile
  literature. | Riots--United States--History--Juvenile literature. |
  Political participation--United States--Juvenile literature. | United
  States--History--Juvenile literature.
Classification: LCC HN57 .S85 2019 | DDC 303.48/40973--dc23
LC record available at https://lccn.loc.gov/2017057875

Printed in the United States of America

CPSIA compliance information: Batch #BS18KL: For further information contact Greenhaven Publishing LLC, New York, New York
at 1-844-317-7404.

Please visit our website, www.greenhavenpublishing.com. For a free color catalog of all
our high-quality books, call toll free 1-844-317-7404 or fax 1-844-317-7405.

Contents

Foreword

The United States is a relatively young country. It has existed as its own nation for more than 200 years, but compared to nations such as China that have existed since ancient times, it is still in its infancy. However, the United States has grown and accomplished much since its birth in 1776. What started as a loose confederation of former British colonies has grown into a major world power whose influence is felt around the globe.

How did the United States manage to develop into a global superpower in such a short time? The answer lies in a close study of its unique history. The story of America is unlike any other—filled with colorful characters, a variety of exciting settings, and events too incredible to be anything other than true.

Too often, the experience of history is lost among the basic facts: names, dates, places, laws, treaties, and battles. These fill countless textbooks, but they are rarely compelling on their own. Far more interesting are the stories that surround those

basic facts. It is in discovering those stories that students are able to see history as a subject filled with life—and a subject that says as much about the present as it does about the past.

The titles in this series allow readers to immerse themselves in the action at pivotal historical moments. They also encourage readers to discuss complex issues in American history—many of which still affect Americans today. These include racism, states' rights, civil liberties, and many other topics that are in the news today but have their roots in the earliest days of America. As such, readers are encouraged to think critically about history and current events.

Each title is filled with excellent tools for research and analysis. Fully cited quotations from historical figures, letters, speeches, and documents provide students with firsthand accounts of major events. Primary sources bring authority to the text, as well. Sidebars highlight these quotes and primary sources, as well as interesting figures and events. Annotated bibliographies allow students to locate and evaluate sources for further information on the subject.

A deep understanding of America's past is necessary to understand its present and its future. Sometimes you have to look back in order to see how to best move forward, and that is certainly true when writing the next chapter in the American story.

1963
On August 28, more than 200,000 people take part in the March on Washington for Jobs and Freedom, which was the civil rights movement's largest event.

1913
On March 3, the Woman's Suffrage Parade in Washington, D.C., occurs. It was the first major march in support of women's right to vote.

1913   1932   1963   1969

1932
Nearly 20,000 World War I veterans with their family members march to Washington, D.C., demanding to be paid their war bonuses.

1969
One of the earliest events of the LGBT+ rights movement, the Stonewall riots take place over a period of six days. The riots were a response to a June 28, 1969, police raid on the Stonewall Inn in New York City's Greenwich Village. On November 15, 500,000 people march to Washington, D.C., to protest the war in Vietnam.

A Timeline

1970
On May 4, nine college students were wounded and four were killed when National Guardsmen opened fire on protesters during a Vietnam War-related protest on the Kent State University campus in Kent, Ohio.

2017
On January 21, more than 3 million people participate in more than 500 Women's March rallies. The largest march in Washington, D.C., included 500,000 participants. It was the largest one-day protest in U.S. history.

2006
More than 1 million immigrants participate in the Great American Boycott (also called a Day without Immigrants), which is an organized national boycott of schools and businesses.

1970	2003	2006	2016	2017

2003
On February 15, protests against the military invasion of Iraq take place in 600 rallies around the world.

2016
From April 2016 to February 2017, millions of people online and in person, along with dozens of Native American groups, support the Standing Rock Sioux tribe's protest of the Dakota Access Pipeline.

Introduction

THE IMPORTANCE OF PROTESTS AND RIOTS

Riots and protests are ways in which people express their opinion on a subject. This dissent—the holding of a different opinion—is most commonly displayed in protests by people who are upset about something that affects their lives, such as an action by a government, an organization, an individual, or society in general. The drive to publicly express personal views has been shared by millions of Americans since the earliest days of the country. These beliefs have led Americans to engage in protests, both peaceful and violent, as well as riots that have destroyed property and injured or killed people. The actions of these protesters have shaped the history of the United States and changed the way its citizens live today.

Protesters sometimes express their opinions on issues in creative ways. In the 1960s, young men who disagreed with the U.S. involvement in the Vietnam

War burned their draft cards. Destroying a draft card was not only an act of protest against the war, but also a crime. Jerry Rubin, famous for unique public protests that often landed him in jail, once traveled with friends to a train depot outside of Oakland, California, and held a sit-in on the train tracks to prevent American troops and supplies from being transported to Vietnam. Sit-ins, or when a group occupies a building or area until the issue of their protest has been addressed, have been a popular form of protest on school campuses for decades.

In *Dissent in America: The Voices That Shaped a Nation*, history professor Ralph F. Young explained that Americans have protested for causes they supported or opposed throughout the nation's history. In the 1960s and early 1970s, the Vietnam War divided the nation. Millions of anti-war protesters made history by convincing the U.S. government to withdraw its troops, and it is often seen as the first war the nation had ever failed to win. Young claimed that protests such as those against the Vietnam War have powerfully influenced the nation. He wrote,

> However we define it, dissent has been the fuel for the engine of American progress. Dissent is central to American history. Not a decade has passed without voices being raised in protest against policies and decisions made by legislators, governors, and presidents. Even before the United States was established, there was dissent.[1]

A Long History of Dissent

One of the most famous early protests took place in Massachusetts Bay Colony in what is now the United States. On December 16, 1773, more than 100 colonists boarded ships in the harbor of Boston, Massachusetts, and dumped 342 chests of tea into the sea. The colonists were protesting the taxes on tea that were imposed on them by the British. Known as the Boston Tea Party, the protest was one of the pivotal incidents that led to the American Revolution in 1775. However, an earlier riot incited by the same anger over taxes also was key in moving the colonists toward revolution.

In 1765, the Stamp Act required colonists to pay a tax on printed material, such as legal or business documents and playing cards. The colonies did not have representation in the British Parliament, which meant that the colonists had no say in whether or how much they would be taxed. The colonists believed it was wrong for Great Britain to tax them without their consent. Citizens in several colonies were so angry that they refused to use the stamps and started riots, destroying the offices and homes of tax officials. There were so many riots that the British government abolished the tax.

Civil rights leader Dr. Martin Luther King Jr. said, "The greatness of America is the right to protest for right."[2] Throughout the nation's history, millions of Americans have shared King's belief by protesting, and sometimes rioting, for various causes. The right to peaceful protest is a right that people in many other countries do not have, which makes the privilege to do so all the more important. By speaking up, millions of Americans have changed the nation in which they live.

The Role of Riots

Hundreds of riots have occurred throughout the history of the United States. Many riots were due to disagreements over politics, while others occurred over social issues, such as divisions between Americans of different races or nationalities. From the end of the American Civil War to the first half of the 20th century, many white Americans rioted against granting equal rights to black Americans. In the 20th century, black and white Americans in many cities protested or rioted in frustration over lack of racial equality for black people.

Riots are frequently disapproved of

A demonstrator is shown here being carried to a police vehicle against her will in Brooklyn, New York, during a 1963 civil rights protest.

because they have resulted in deaths and injuries as well as widespread property destruction. In *Rioting in America*, however, history professor Paul A. Gilje explained that some of those episodes of violence helped shape the United States in a positive manner. Gilje wrote,

> Rioting is part of the American past. All too often riots are seen as brief moments of spontaneous collective violence that erupt unto the scene, but only temporarily interrupt the constant and peaceful pulse of American politics and society …
>
> Riots have been important mechanisms for change. In the story of America, popular disorder has expressed social discontent, altered economic arrangement, affected politics, and toppled regimes. Without an understanding of the impact of rioting, we cannot fully comprehend the history of the American people.[3]

Despite the violence and lawless

African American students are shown here marching past demonstrators carrying pro-segregation signs.

activities that are associated with riots, some riots have played key roles in shaping the nation. The anger and spontaneity of riots is a reflection of emotions about important issues. In this way, riots and protests represent a large part of the history of the American people. The Stamp Act riots marked the beginning of the open revolt of the colonists against British rule. The Boston Tea Party pushed the country closer to a revolution. The lynching riots of the segregated South revealed ugly truths about the consequences of Jim Crow laws. The Black Lives Matter protests woke Americans up to the realities of police brutality.

Whether someone is a protester, activist, journalist, politician, victim, or perpetrator, it is important to remember that protests and riots affect many people, and those people have very real needs, emotions, motivations, and goals that others should try to understand.

Chapter One

SAME AS IT EVER WAS

Protests and riots have taken place throughout history. From protesting for women's voting rights to protesting against segregation, people have protested about things they are passionate about and things that greatly affect their lives. Just as the reasons for protesting are varied, the methods of protesting are as well. From sit-ins to marches, people throughout history have fought hard for their rights, even in present times.

Not Afraid to Speak

Protesters and rioters are often alike in that they are not afraid to risk offending someone by expressing their point of view or by doing so loudly or in a way that involves breaking the law. In 1872, a group of women that included Susan B. Anthony protested in support of women's suffrage by gathering to vote in Rochester, New York. Anthony was arrested two weeks later, convicted of breaking voting laws, and fined $100. (In 2017, this amount would be equivalent to $2,000.) Anthony felt that she had to go to such lengths, including committing a crime, to bring attention to the issue. She explained,

> Cautious, careful people, always looking about to preserve their reputation and social standing, never can bring about a reform. Those who are really in earnest must be willing to be anything or nothing in the world's estimation, and publicly and privately, in season and out, avow their sympathy with despised and persecuted ideas and their advocates, and bear the consequences.[4]

Other women who defied authority to gain the right to vote picketed at the gates of the White House in 1917 and were arrested for allegedly endangering

In 1869, Susan B. Anthony (shown here) and Elizabeth Cady Stanton founded the National Woman Suffrage Association to help women win the right to vote.

traffic with their peaceful organized protest. The dramatic efforts of Anthony and other women helped force the United States to add the 19th Amendment to the U.S. Constitution in 1920 to grant women the right to vote. Both Anthony and the White House protesters were willing to risk arrest to accomplish goals they believed in. They were acting out the philosophy of civil disobedience, which involves breaking laws to protest something someone believes is wrong. The principles of civil disobedience were perfected by philosopher Henry David Thoreau in the late 1840s.

In 1846, Thoreau was jailed for failing to pay a local tax in Concord, Massachusetts. He refused to pay the tax as a protest of slavery and the 1846 decision by the United States to go to war against Mexico. He only spent one night in jail because an unidentified person paid Thoreau's tax bill for him. Two years later, on January 26, 1848, Thoreau gave a speech about the principle of civil disobedience that he had used when he refused to pay the tax. According to Thoreau, it was better for people to break unjust laws than to follow them because the laws might harm other people. He explained,

Unjust laws exist: shall we be content to obey them, or shall we endeavor to amend them, and obey them until we have succeeded, or shall we transgress them at once? …

[If the evil of a law] is of such a nature that it requires you to be the agent of injustice to another, then, I say, break the law … I do not lend myself to the wrong which I condemn.[5]

Thoreau's *On the Duty of Civil Disobedience* is seen today as a manifesto for non-violent protest. Mahatma Gandhi, César Chávez, and Martin Luther King Jr. all considered it essential reading. Originally titled "Resistance to Civil Government," it argued that conscience can be a higher authority than government and that "under a government that imprisons unjustly, the true place for a just man is also a prison."[6] Many people have agreed with Thoreau and have been jailed as a result of protesting a government policy they did not agree with. Civil disobedience has also been used many times to protest wars, including World War I, World War II, and the Vietnam War. In his autobiography, King explained that Thoreau's writing convinced him he was right to fight for equal rights for African Americans even if it meant breaking laws perceived as racist, such as those that forced black people to live under segregation in southern states. King wrote of Thoreau: "No other person has been more eloquent and passionate in getting this idea across than Henry David Thoreau. As a result of his writings and personal witness, we are the heirs of a legacy of creative protest."[7]

Methods of Speaking Out

There are many ways people can protest things they believe are wrong. One of the simplest and most effective is to gather

Tax Resistance as a War Protest

Citizens have refused to pay taxes as a protest to every single war America has been involved in, and a few before the United States declared independence from Great Britain in 1776. Soon after arriving in the colonies, the pacifist, or peaceful, Quakers were known for their war tax protests. During the American Revolution, Quakers were jailed and their property was seized and auctioned off as a punishment for war tax resistance. After the American Revolution, Quakers continued this cycle of protest and punishment because their taxes went toward paying off war debt. It was not until World War II, however, that the government authorized a permanent U.S. military, and so it was not until then that war tax resistance became a mass movement. In 1942, Ernest Bromley refused payment of $7.09 for a defense tax stamp required for his cars and was jailed for 60 days. His story angered war tax protesters to action. The number of income tax resisters grew from 275 in 1966 to about 20,000 in the 1970s in the wake of the Vietnam War.

people in one place to demonstrate the scale of people who support a similar cause. These gatherings can take place at public events, such as town hall meetings, or in the form of protest marches or large gatherings where the assembled crowd listens to speeches about the issue they are rallying around. Labor unions have regularly protested low wages or other contract disputes by picketing, which often involves marching in front of their employer's business while carrying signs stating their complaints. People protesting other causes have also picketed.

Some of the largest and most historic protests have taken place in the nation's capital, Washington, D.C. One such protest was the March on Washington for Jobs and Freedom on August 28, 1963, in which people rallied against racial discrimination. Martin Luther King Jr. spoke to the crowd of 250,000 people, explaining his dream of a nation in which black people would no longer face discrimination because of their skin color. In plain but elegant words, King said, "I have a dream that my four children will one day live in a nation where they will not be judged by the color of their skin but by the content of their character."[8]

Many years later, another march on Washington, D.C., was organized, but this time it was for science. In 2017, President Donald Trump announced that his goals for the country's 2018 budget would include a significant decrease in funding for the Environmental Protection Agency (EPA), National Institutes of

Health (NIH), Centers for Disease Control and Prevention (CDC), Department of Energy, and National Aeronautics and Space Administration (NASA). Some of the Trump administration's immigration policies also affected dozens of scientists, doctors, and doctoral candidates, including researchers for diseases such as human immunodeficiency virus (HIV), acquired immunodeficiency syndrome (AIDS), Ebola, and tuberculosis. In response, many scientists took to social media to express their worries and outrage. The March for Science began as an idea after the Women's March on Washington in January 2017. The resulting mass protest by scientists took place in more than 600 locations with thousands of protesters. Neuroscientist David Badre was one of the protesters and voiced his opinion on the protest and events that inspired it:

> *A couple of years ago if you asked me if I would go to a march for science, I would have thought of it in the same way as a march for sound airplanes, or ... a march for well-built bridges—it's not like society really needs it ... [but recently] there's been a devaluation of evidence-based policy and decision-making.*[9]

Aside from the new methods of organization that involved using technology such as social media, the March for Science was no different than many other marches that had taken place throughout the nation's history. Like other protests throughout American history, those who participated were motivated by the same desire—to publicly express their point of view on an issue they deeply cared about.

Mass public protests are frequently effective because they attract attention and demonstrate the strength of support for a specific issue. However, protesters can demonstrate their collective strength by having thousands and even millions of people sign petitions or write letters to public officials for their cause, whether related to ending a war, allowing gay and lesbian people to marry, or lowering taxes. Protests by individuals or small groups can also be effective.

Individuals and Groups Standing Their Ground

Protesters have found many creative ways to make statements about their beliefs. In 1960, African Americans in southern cities staged sit-ins at "whites only" restaurants that refused to serve them. These protesters sat in seats for hours without being served, and many were arrested.

Environmental activists have sometimes acted alone to try to stop construction projects they believe will endanger the natural habitats of animals. Activists have chained themselves to trees, gates, or bulldozers. Individuals who oppose the use of animal fur for clothing have tossed paint on people wearing fur coats.

Protesters who opposed the 2003 invasion of Iraq, which was led by the United States, and other armed conflicts have staged die-ins in which

Protests at Construction Sites

The largest gathering of indigenous nations in history occurred in 2016 in a show of support for the Sioux Native American group of Standing Rock, North Dakota, as they protested construction of an oil pipeline across their sacred tribal land. The #NoDAPL (referencing the Dakota Access Pipeline) movement gained worldwide media attention and drew thousands of protesters to the site. A number of major confrontations took place between the police and protesters. Several protesters were bitten by security dogs, while others were shot with water cannons on a below-freezing November day. Dozens of protesters were arrested throughout the months of protest. The pipeline was built in 2017, but Linda Black Elk, a member of the Standing Rock Sioux group, said of the protests: "A year and a half ago we were invisible, we were invisible people ... we were invisible to people. They didn't want to see us and we're not invisible anymore."[1]

1. Quoted in Dan Gunderson, "'Not Invisible Anymore': Standing Rock a Year After Pipeline Protests," MPRNews, September 13, 2017. www.mprnews.org/story/2017/09/13/standing-rock-nd-a-year-after-oil-pipeline-protests.

As a direct response to the Standing Rock protests, South Dakota's governor signed a bill prohibiting groups of more than 20 people from gathering on state land. The bill also criminalized protests on state highways.

In 2011, several hundred protesters in New York City began a sit-in over the mortgage crisis, financial corruption, and economic inequality. Some camped in Manhattan's Zuccotti Park for months. Mass arrests of protesters, who called their movement Occupy Wall Street, made the news every week.

they pretended to be dead, with some wearing bandages or simulated blood to make them look more like real war casualties.

Young claimed that in more than two centuries of protesting, "American dissenters have achieved different levels of success … [by] hammering away at the powers-that-be until those powers began to listen, public opinion was swayed, laws were made."[10] Young cited major victories achieved by protesters, including unions being allowed to organize to better the lives of workers, African Americans being granted equal rights, women being granted the right to vote, gays and lesbians being granted the right to marry, and the 13 colonies being able to govern themselves.

Violence and Chaos

Some protests have been marred by violence and at times have exploded into full-fledged riots. When the Democratic National Convention was held in Chicago, Illinois, in August 1968 to select

Hunger Strikes

Hunger strikes have been a form of protest for a long time. These strikes have no direct effect on the intended target but instead place an emphasis on the protester's own life as they support or reject a cause. As the protester suffers, they are relying on morality and emotions to cause sway, as well as gaining publicity for their cause. Hunger strikes were popular among suffragettes who had been jailed for protesting because in jail there are few other ways to continue a protest. Union leader and civil rights activist César Chávez staged several fasts, the first of which lasted for 25 days in 1968.

the party's presidential candidate for the upcoming election, 10,000 people, most of them college or high school students, went to the convention to protest the Vietnam War. These protests began peacefully but developed into several days of full-scale rioting when police, soldiers, and members of the National Guard wielding batons and shooting tear gas canisters used what many believed to be excessive force to control the protesters. In a similar manner, peaceful civil rights marches by African Americans in the 1960s turned into riots when white people, including law enforcement officials who did not want black people to have equal rights, attacked protesters.

However, such violence did not begin with the protests of the 1960s. Late historian Richard C. Wade stated, "Violence is no stranger to American cities. Almost from the very beginning, cities have been the scenes of sporadic violence, of rioting

and disorders, and occasionally virtual rebellion against established authority."[11] Examples of violent protests include the 1765 Stamp Act riots, the physical battles between labor unions and management in the 19th and 20th centuries, and two centuries of racial conflicts between white and black Americans.

Riots

The first step to understanding riots is to define the term, which is not easy because a riot involves more than an outbreak of violence. In *Rioting in America*, Gilje provided this definition: "[A] riot is any group of twelve or more people attempting to assert their will immediately through the use of force outside the normal bounds of law."[12] Even Gilje admitted his definition is subject to interpretation because the level of force people use, whether they are shouting obscenities, beating or killing others, or damaging property, determines how much criminal conduct is involved.

Riots, however, do not simply happen out of nowhere. Law professors David D. Haddock and Daniel D. Polsby claimed that every riot springs from an event that creates strong emotions in people. In their article, "Understanding Riots," they wrote,

> As word spreads of a conventional triggering event—whether it is shocking (like an assassination) or rhapsodic [a championship for a local sports team]—crowds form spontaneously in various places, without any one person having to recruit them.[13]

An example of such an event occurred in New York City in 1969 when police raided the Stonewall Inn, a popular gathering place for gay men, and began arresting people even though they were not breaking any laws. The arrests ignited lingering anger in the LGBT+ community about past mistreatment by police and caused members of the community to fight back. This sparked the Stonewall riots, a landmark event in the history of the fight for LGBT+ rights.

Another factor that leads to riots are strong emotions that cause participants to perform acts they would never normally do, such as destroying property or beating or killing people. Such emotions can spring from anger over an incident, such as the 1968 assassination of Martin Luther King Jr., to the happiness sports fans feel when their team wins a big game. When the Los Angeles Lakers won the National Basketball Association (NBA) championship on June 14, 2009, excited fans celebrated outside the Staples Center arena where the Lakers had played. Soon, the fans' emotions were out of control, and some damaged police cars, threw rocks and bottles at police officers, and lit fires. Gilje said that when crowds get pumped up by such strong feelings, "the normal rules of society are put aside," and people are more prone to abnormal behavior. He explained that for people caught up in such a situation,

> [r]ioting was not a daily routine. Each participant in a riot knew that he was involved in an exceptional episode of his life. Emotions and passions surfaced; people got carried away with what they were doing. Normally reserved individuals might find themselves cheering on the tarring and feathering [of another person], or, worse, firing away at the helpless victim themselves.[14]

The looting of stores during riots is an example of the type of criminal action that strong emotions can lead people to perform. In the 1960s, Vietnam War protests on college campuses often resulted in the destruction of school property. When many rallies ended, the protesters leaving them were so angry over the war that their emotions led them to destructive acts such as breaking windows, smashing doors, and damaging other property. Many of the people who performed such

Martin Luther King Jr. provided a voice for many people and headed a movement that many believed in. When he was assassinated in 1968, riots broke out, including in Washington D.C., which is shown here.

acts would never have done anything like that on their own but became caught up in the frenzy of an angry crowd and joined in the destruction.

The addition of people who like to cause trouble makes it more likely that protests will erupt into riots. However, the anger people have about an issue may often be enough to make passionate supporters of a cause act violently and commit destructive criminal acts they would ordinarily not have done.

Protesters Become Heroes

Like rioters, many people involved in protests have been condemned because the beliefs they expressed were unpopular. However, as time passed, many of the beliefs protesters held became accepted by a majority of Americans.

For example, the abolition of slavery was not a public cause in America until the Second Great Awakening of the 1700s and 1800s. The religious movement of the Second Great Awakening led people to fully support abolition based on moral grounds. Slaves, abolitionists explained, were humans, too, and deserved to be treated well and paid for their work.

Over time, many protesters who were

The United States Postal Service frequently issues stamps that honor prominent Americans, including the protest leaders shown here.

criticized by national leaders and other citizens were transformed from villains to heroes. Martin Luther King Jr., who was bitterly hated by many white people while fighting for equality for African Americans, is now honored with a national holiday on the third Monday of January every year. Susan B. Anthony, who fought for women's right to vote, was honored with a U.S. commemorative stamp in 1936 and a dollar coin in 1979.

Chapter Two

VOCAL CITIZENS

Many of the protests and riots that have occurred throughout U.S. history have been directed against the government. The nation itself evolved out of the dissent of its own citizens. Protests and riots during the colonial era, such as the Boston Tea Party, led directly to the American Revolution. From this battle emerged the United States, a nation that was committed to allowing its citizens a say in how they were governed—and not long after the nation was created, its citizens used this power to oppose government actions with which they disagreed.

Rebellion in a Young Country

In 1786, Daniel Shays led more than 1,200 farmers in an armed protest in central and western Massachusetts that became known as Shays's Rebellion. The rebellious farmers tried to seize control of local government to protest high taxes, a poor economy, and a financial system that had burdened farmers and other people with huge debts they could not repay. A primary goal of the protest was to stop courts from allowing lenders to take land from farmers or put them in debtor's prison if they could not pay their debts. The rebellion lasted from August 1786 to February 1787, when a state militia arrested Shays and more than 1,000 others.

Future U.S. president Thomas Jefferson believed it was admirable that the farmers had taken up arms against a government they believed was treating them unfairly. He wrote, "I hold it that a little rebellion now and then is a good thing, and as necessary in the political world as storms in the physical ... God forbid we should ever be twenty years without such a rebellion."[15]

In 1788, a general amnesty was declared for Shays and most other participants in his rebellion. Like many other protests and riots in U.S. history, Shays's Rebellion resulted in changes that made the nation stronger and a better place to live.

Creation of the Constitution

Shays's Rebellion revealed a truth about America's young government: It needed a better set of rules for governing than the Articles of Confederation, which the colonies had adopted during the American Revolution. The articles failed to give enough power to the federal government to perform the tasks necessary to make the individual states a true nation, such as regulating commerce between states and having a unified court system. When the farmers revolted, the federal government had no power to intercede in state matters, and Massachusetts had to raise an army to stop them. To correct this flaw, state representatives met for a Constitutional Convention in Philadelphia, Pennsylvania, in May 1787.

After months of vigorous debate, 39 out of 55 delegates signed the U.S. Constitution on September 17, 1787. This historic document created the federal government as it exists today with an executive branch led by a president, a national judicial system headed by the U.S. Supreme Court, and a legislative branch consisting of representatives from each state. It was a bold departure from how most countries were ruled by kings or other members of royalty.

However, many people were concerned that the Constitution gave too much power to the federal government over states and individuals. To ease these fears, a bill of rights was added to the Constitution that guaranteed people basic freedoms that the new, stronger federal government could never deny them. On December 15, 1791, the states approved the Bill of Rights in the form of 10 amendments to the Constitution.

The First Amendment to the Constitution guarantees crucial freedoms. It reads,

> *Congress shall make no law respecting an establishment of religion, or prohibiting the free exercise thereof; or abridging the freedom of speech, or of the press; or the right of the people peaceably to assemble, and to petition the Government for a redress of grievances.*[16]

The First Amendment assures citizens that they have the right to disagree publicly with what the government does and demand changes they believe necessary, such as lowering taxes, ending a war, or giving women the right to vote. This right, and the fact that any power the government has stems from the people and not from its elected officials, has empowered U.S. citizens to freely, openly, and sometimes violently voice their displeasure with their government. Americans have since been able to exercise their rights on nearly any issue imaginable. One of the common targets is taxation and how the government spends tax dollars.

How Emotions and Ideas Spread

In 1765, Great Britain created the Stamp Act, which required every type of written material to have a tax stamp, or British seal, which colonists had to pay to obtain. A group known as the Sons of Liberty used violence to protest this tax. In many cities, the Sons of Liberty damaged and looted the offices and homes of tax officials. Sometimes, they coated government officials with tar and chicken feathers, a practice known as tarring and feathering. This type of assault was painful and sometimes resulted in serious burns or even death for the victims. Thomas Hutchinson witnessed hundreds of people ransacking Boston during one riot in response to the Stamp Act. Hutchinson recalled, "The town was, the whole night, under awe of this mob; many of the magistrates, with the field officers of the militia, standing by as spectators; and no body daring to oppose [them]."[17]

Late historian Page Smith claimed that anger over the tax stamps was so widespread that it united colonists in an unprecedented way. Smith wrote,

The evidence is in the rhetoric. In the space of a few weeks the colonists stopped talking of "our colony" or "our province" and began speaking of "our poor degraded country," and

When Great Britain created the Stamp Act, it was wildly unpopular. One Stamp Act protest is shown here, and people protested in other ways as well. For example, colonial women boycotted British imports, such as tea, and made their own fabric.

of themselves as "Americans." For the first time a current of sympathy and mutual affection flowed from colony to colony. Ideas and actions spawned in one province were quickly and enthusiastically adopted in another.[18]

Colonists were united so strongly that on November 1, 1765, the day the tax began, no items requiring tax stamps were sold. The boycott weakened Great Britain's economy so much that in March 1766, it repealed the tax, giving colonists a huge victory and showing them how powerful they could be when they acted together.

A People Ready to Rule Themselves

Another historic tax protest was the Boston Tea Party on December 16, 1773. Angry that Britain was taxing tea, 5,000 people gathered in Boston, Massachusetts, to show their displeasure. That night, more than 100 Sons of Liberty protesters boarded 3 tea ships docked in the harbor and threw several tons of tea into the sea. This illegal act led to the creation of new laws to punish Massachusetts residents. Anger over the tax and the disciplinary laws spread throughout the colonies, and the American Revolution began two years later.

The Boston Tea Party has been an enduring symbol of citizen outrage over taxation for more than two centuries.

Extreme Measures

The Great Depression, which started in 1929, put tens of millions of people out of work and was the worst economic crisis in U.S. history. In 1932, veterans of World War I went to Washington, D.C., to demand payment of a bonus the federal government had promised them in 1924 for fighting in the war. The bonus was not due to them until 1945, but the men, many of them unemployed and living in poverty, claimed they needed the money right away to survive.

The first disgruntled veterans of the protest group, known as the Bonus Army, arrived on May 23. Many carried U.S. flags or signs demanding the bonus that was due to them or a job. During the spring and summer of 1932, nearly 20,000 veterans—and their wives and children—came to the nation's capital to plead for the bonus. They camped at several sites near the Capitol, and some of them occupied vacant buildings. The largest group of more than 10,000 took up residence in an uninhabited swampy area known as the Anacostia Flats. They slept in shelters made from old lumber and boxes with roofs of scrap tin or straw scavenged from a nearby trash dump. Most veterans had little or no money, and they survived on food donated by local charities. The group's leader, Walter Waters, a former U.S. Army sergeant from Portland, Oregon, said, "We're here for the duration and we're not going to starve … If the Bonus is paid it will relieve to a large extent the deplorable economic condition [of veterans]."[19]

The general public looked favorably on their plea for economic help, but some elected officials were not sympathetic. U.S. Representative Wright Patman of Texas proposed a bill to pay the bonuses, which totaled $2.4 billion. On June 15, the U.S. House of Representatives passed the bill with 211–176 votes, but 2 days later, the U.S. Senate rejected it 62–18. When members of the Bonus Army vowed to remain in Washington, D.C., until the bonus was due in 1945, officials began to lose their patience. Finally, on July 28, 1932, the federal government asked police to force the veterans to leave. When the veterans resisted, police shot and killed two of them but failed to force the rest of them out. President Herbert Hoover then ordered the army to remove the veterans in what became the most powerful use of military force ever used against protesting U.S. citizens.

More than 200 mounted cavalry soldiers, 300 infantry soldiers, and 5 tanks charged into the areas where protesters were staying, clearing them out with brute force and the use of tear gas. The action was so unpopular with Americans that Franklin D. Roosevelt, the governor of New York at the time and who was considering a run for president, predicted, "This will elect me."[20] Thanks partly to anger over the harsh treatment of veterans by Republican President Hoover, on November 8, Roosevelt, a Democrat, won the presidential election. Although the Bonus Army was initially defeated, Congress authorized the bonuses two years later to give the veterans a delayed victory.

Grenades and tanks were used to attack a Bonus Army encampment, shown here.

The Disability Rights Movement

The disability rights movement began in April 1977 in San Francisco, California, when more than 100 people occupied the city's federal building for 25 days. The protesters refused to vacate the building until Section 504 of the Rehabilitation Act of 1973 was signed into law, which would make it illegal for federally-fund-ed facilities and programs to discriminate against people with disabilities. They wanted laws to protect their rights just like other groups, such as African Americans, had been granted. This protest is the longest takeover of a federal building in the country's history.

The Emergency 504 Coalition organized the sit-in in advance, setting up committees to make sure that medi-

A Tragedy Against Veterans

On July 28, 1932, President Herbert Hoover ordered the U.S. Army to force thousands of men who were members of the Bonus Army and their families to vacate the nation's capital. His decision resulted in the largest use of military force against U.S. citizens in history. An article in *Smithsonian* magazine described how the soldiers forced the Bonus Army to leave:

> *For the first time in the nation's history, tanks rolled through the streets of the capital … At 4:30 p.m., nearly 200 mounted cavalry, sabers drawn and pennants flying, wheeled out … At the head of this [group] rode their executive officer, George S. Patton, followed by five tanks and about 300 helmeted infantrymen, brandishing loaded rifles with fixed bayonets. The cavalry drove most pedestrians—curious onlookers, civil servants and members of the Bonus Army; many with wives and children—off the streets. Infantrymen wearing gas masks hurled hundreds of tear-gas grenades at the dispersing crowd. The detonated grenades set off dozens of fires: the flimsy shelters veterans had erected near the armory went up in flames. Black clouds mingled with tear gas …*
>
> *By 7:00 p.m., soldiers had evacuated the entire downtown encampment—perhaps as many as 2,000 men, women and children—along with countless bystanders. By 9:00, these troops were crossing the bridge to Anacostia …*
>
> *The troops swooped down on Camp Marks, driving off some 2,000 veterans with tear gas and setting fire to the camp, which quickly burned.*[1]

1. Paul Dickson and Thomas B. Allen, "Marching on History," *Smithsonian*, February 2003. www.smithsonianmag.com/history/marching-on-history-75797769/.

cal, food, publicity, and other needs were met. They received support from labor unions, LGBT+ rights organizations, and many others. Several politicians sent mattresses and a shower hose to attach to the sink for the protesters to use. San Francisco's Glide Memorial Church and the Black Panther party, a revolutionary African American groupy, organized food for the protesters. Media was carefully organized around a series of messages that had been voted on by the Emergency

504 Coalition. Throughout the sit-in, protesters sang freedom songs, both for the morale boost and to show the media that this event was directly connected to the civil rights movement. The International Association of Machinists sent 12 delegates to Washington, D.C., during the sit-in to speak with elected officials, and they hosted the group at their international headquarters during their stay. While in Washington, D.C., they blocked the door to every event then-President Jimmy Carter attended throughout the city.

Wade Blank marched with Martin Luther King Jr. in the famous Selma, Alabama, civil rights movement marches, and he brought many lessons about protesting with him to Denver, Colorado. He and residents of the independent living home he founded, named Atlantis Community, formed an activist group called ADAPT (American Disabled for Accessible Public Transit, although as of 2017 it stands for American Disabled for Attendant Programs Today). Blank was greatly influenced by the militancy and attention-getting power of black power groups, which also informed ADAPT's acts. ADAPT members traveled across the country protesting for access to public transit. Many protesters were arrested, though they could not be moved to jails because there was no accessible transportation. Police often resorted to detaining them in their wheelchairs behind makeshift barricades.

In 1978, a group of disabled people in Denver, who would come to be known as the Gang of 19, threw themselves in front of buses to protest the lack of access to public transit. They had tried to negotiate with the transit authority for more than a year to no benefit. In protest, they blocked the street, chanting that they would ride and causing a major traffic jam for two days as they refused to move.

With the national attention of the Denver protest adding to their confidence, ADAPT demanded access laws, staging protests at restaurants, schools, colleges, post offices, and more. Wade Blank's experience in protesting led to many powerful protests that greatly affected legislators. In 1980, they took sledgehammers to Denver's curbs protesting for access to sidewalks. Colorado would be the first state to have accessible public transportation and accessible sidewalks with ramps. When they protested at the American Public Transportation Association's national convention, they blocked access to the street, forcing attendees to climb over them to leave. In 1990, they left their wheelchairs behind to crawl up the steps of the Capitol Building in Washington, D.C., to protest for the Americans with Disabilities Act.

After achieving the passage of new laws in support of their cause, ADAPT turned its attention to health care policies and Medicaid. In 2017, nine protesters were arrested in Denver Senator Cory Gardner's office after occupying his office's lobby for 57 hours. This was one of many acts of protest they made against cuts to Medicaid funding. ADAPT has continued to travel around the country holding sit-ins and and other

More than 200 ADAPT protestors blocked the sidewalks in front of the White House in 2013 to gain attention for their protests against health care cuts.

protests in politicians offices. At a June 2017 ADAPT protest against Medicaid cuts in Rochester, New York, 25 people were arrested. National ADAPT organizer Bruce Darling said, "this country wasn't founded by a group of people who held a press conference and said the king was unjust."[21] Colorado Cross-Disability Coalition Executive Director Julie Reiskin said this about ADAPT: "I see ADAPT's role kind of where it's always been as the people who are willing to go to the mat when needed and engage in nonviolent civil disobedience when needed. They're really representing all of (the disabled community)."[22]

The Prisoners' Rights Movement

The 1970s also saw the rise of the movement for prisoners' rights. In 1866, the U.S. Supreme Court ruled in *Pervear v. Massachusetts* that prisoners had no constitutional nor personal rights because they were convicted of a crime. It was not until the 1960s that

Nuclear Resistance

Nuclear weapons and nuclear energy were protested by a growing group in the 1960s and early 1970s. On November 1, 1961, around 50,000 women in 60 worldwide cities participated in Women Strike for Peace marches against nuclear bomb testing. A small group of islands in the Pacific called the Bikini Atoll had been

Activists' concerns were proven to be correct with the Three Mile Island disaster. Four activists are shown here at the Three Mile Island site in 1979.

the U.S. Supreme Court decided that prisoners had some rights. Wilbert Rideau, who was an inmate in Louisiana's Angola State Penitentiary for decades, explained prison protests in the *New York Times*:

There aren't many protests in prison. In a world where authorities exercise absolute power and demand abject obedience, prisoners are almost always going to be on the losing side, and they know it …

forever abandoned because of the bomb testing done there. Nuclear resistance leader Dagmar Wilson said, "I decided that there are some things the individual citizen can do … At least we can make some noise and see. If we are going to have to go under, I don't want to have to go under without a shout."[1]

Tragically, the movement gained ground because of a nuclear disaster. In March 1979, the Three Mile Island nuclear power plant in Pennsylvania had a partial nuclear meltdown, and radioactive matter leaked into the local environment. The activists, who had been accused of exaggerating, preying on people's fears, and being uninformed, were suddenly right. Within a month, more than 65,000 people marched in Washington, D.C., to protest nuclear energy. Nearly 200,000 people gathered to protest the same issue in New York City in September, one of a dozen cities to host an anti-nuclear protest on the same day. In Vernon, Vermont, the protest ended with the arrest of 187 demonstrators for trespassing at a local nuclear plant. Actress and activist Jane Fonda told the New York City protesters:

> We believe all of us against nuclear energy have to think of ourselves as Paul Reveres [a colonialist who warned the colonial militia of the approach of the British in 1775] and Pauline Reveres, going through our country town by town, city by city warning the people about the dangers.[2]

1. Quoted in Dennis Hevesi, "Dagmar Wilson, Anti-Nuclear Leader, Dies at 94," *New York Times*, January 23, 2011. www.nytimes.com/2011/01/24/us/24wilson.html.

2. Quoted in Robin Herman, "Nearly 200,000 Rally to Protest Nuclear Energy," *New York Times*, September 24, 1979. nytimes.com/1979/09/24/archives/nearly-200000-rally-to-protest-nuclear-energy-gathering-at-the.html.

And yet, sometimes things get so bad that prisoners feel compelled to protest, with work stoppages, riots or hunger strikes.[23]

It took a big event such as the 1971 Attica Prison Riot for this civil rights issue to become a movement. For years, inmates incarcerated in Attica Correctional Facility in Attica, New York, had tried to go through proper channels to get enough food to eat, clean facilities, and less crowding, but they were not listened to. By 1971, they had enough—more than 1,200 inmates held 39 prison staff members hostage to force the governor to negotiate with them. The prisoners elected leaders, drafted demands, and began preparing first aid and food for themselves and their hostages. Several days passed without any violence when suddenly New York State governor Nelson Rockefeller abruptly stopped negotiations. He sent 600 heavily armed troops into the prison, and 29 prisoners and 10 hostages were killed in a hail of bullets and tear gas. Order was restored, and better medical care and food, less mail censorship, and parole reform would eventually somewhat improve prison conditions. There were negative consequences to the protest, however, as Heather Ann Thompson, the historian whose 11 years of research led to exposure of a massive cover-up of the Attica riot by Rockefeller, pointed out:

> While prisoners may be paying penance, they are still human beings deserving of basic rights. In the wake of the Attica prison uprising, Americans began voting for ever-more punitive laws, incarceration rates skyrocketed, and the public felt little empathy for anyone who ended up in jail or prison.[24]

In 1973, the Oklahoma State Prison at McAlester was burned down by another prison riot over living conditions. The prison was at double the capacity it was built for, segregation and discrimination decided housing and job assignments, cells were dark and filthy, officers often used tear gas and mace in retaliation for small offenses, and there was little medical care. Earlier that year, prisoners staged a hunger strike to bring attention to these issues, but they were ignored. After the riot, Oklahoma's Department of Corrections was soon forced to make serious changes.

In 2013, 30,000 California inmates started a hunger strike to protest the use of solitary confinement. This was their third hunger strike for this cause in two years. It took 60 days and 1 death before lawmakers agreed to hear their demands. In 2016, frustrated inmates in 23 states participated in another prison strike. Their demands were similar to the Attica prisoners' demands, and they began the strike on the 45th anniversary of the 1971 uprising. Mike Smith, one of the guards who was held hostage, pointed out that "when you put a problem behind walls it is sort of as if society doesn't have to look at it or acknowledge it until there is a riot."[25]

Chapter Three

PROTESTING WAR

John Adams, a leader of the colonists during the American Revolution and the second president of the United States, said, "The Revolution was effected before the War commenced. The Revolution was in the Minds and Hearts of the People."[26] Adams meant that even before colonists began fighting Great Britain for independence in 1775, they believed they had the right to protest government actions if they thought those actions were harmful. This belief has led Americans to continue protesting government actions for more than two centuries.

Adams claimed that at least one-third of colonists opposed the American Revolution. Opponents included people sympathetic to ongoing British rule and members of religious groups, such as the Quakers who oppose all wars and violence.

Opposition to wars only continued from there. During the Civil War, the United States needed so many soldiers to fight for the Union that for the first time it had to draft civilians to fight. In July 1863, when the government began naming men for the draft, many violent protests broke out. Much of the violence occurred in New York City, where rioters damaged draft offices, public buildings, and the homes of city officials and Republican party leaders.

During the Vietnam War in the 1960s and 1970s, tens of millions of people protested the nation's involvement in the conflict. Historian Howard Zinn wrote,

This was the greatest movement against war in the nation's history. On October 15, 1969, perhaps two million people across the nation gathered not only in the big cities, but in towns and villages that had never seen an anti-war demonstration.[27]

A march that was part of the Moratorium to End the War in Vietnam, which took place a month later on November 15, 1969, was the largest anti-war protest in U.S. history. Protesters that day were doing what Americans had for nearly two centuries—opposing their nation's involvement in a war.

Opposing the Draft

The issue of slavery divided the nation, resulting in the Civil War. The fierce fighting killed and wounded so many men that President Abraham Lincoln was forced to sign the Conscription Act on March 3, 1863, to draft men into military service. A draft forces civilians into military service. However, men who were drafted could hire a substitute to replace them or purchase an exemption for $300. Some people opposed the draft because they believed it was unfair to allow wealthy people to buy their way out of the war or because they did not think the government had the right to force anyone to join the army.

When the United States entered World War I in 1917, so many Americans were against the idea of joining the war that the government once again had to draft soldiers. Georgia Senator Thomas Hardwick said, "There was undoubtedly general and widespread opposition on the part of many thousands … to the enactment of the draft law … and largely attended mass meetings in every part of the States protested against it."[28] Even though the federal government passed a law making it illegal to oppose the war, about 900 people were jailed for speaking against the conflict. In addition, more than 330,000 men avoided the draft so they would not have to go to war. In Oklahoma, 450 members of the Socialist Party and International Workers of the World labor union were jailed for planning a march to the nation's capital to protest the draft. Sentences for the men ranged from 60 days in jail to 10 years for the leaders of the planned protest.

The Japanese attack on Pearl Harbor in Hawai'i on December 7, 1941, made most Americans eager to fight in World War II. Although 10 million men were drafted, only 43,000 refused to fight in the war, and 6,000 men were imprisoned for refusing to join the armed forces.

The War Most Protested

The Vietnam War was fought from 1954 to 1975 between Communist North Vietnam and democratic South Vietnam for control of both nations. In the late 1950s, the United States, as part of its global battle against communism, began sending military advisers to South Vietnam to train its army to fight North Vietnam. In 1964, President Lyndon B. Johnson began sending more soldiers to help South Vietnam fight because it was losing the war. When

Johnson boosted the number of soldiers there from 23,000 in 1965 to more than 500,000 by 1968, he ignited the fiercest anti-war opposition the United States had ever seen. Protesters invented new ways to oppose war.

Many people once again protested the draft. When men turned 18, they were required by law to register for the draft. They then received draft cards that they were supposed to carry at all times. At anti-war rallies, young men set their draft cards on fire, holding the burning documents high as a symbol

During the Vietnam War, many American men were arrested for burning their draft cards. Some men protested by refusing to register for the draft or for refusing to report for the medical examination to see if they were physically fit to be drafted.

On May 17, 1968, a group of people who became known as the Catonsville Nine took nearly 400 draft files from a government office in Catonsville, Maryland, and set them on fire with homemade napalm. One of the burglars was Daniel Berrigan (center), a Jesuit priest.

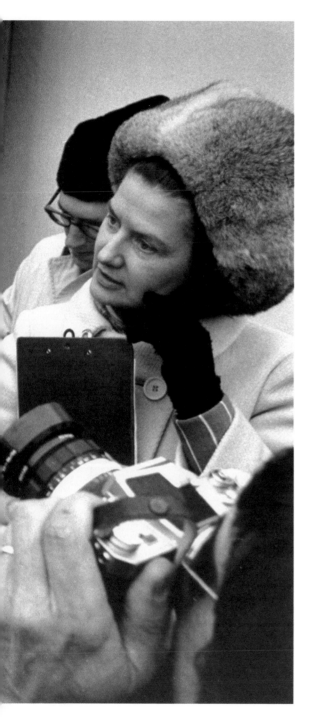

of resistance. One resister, Philip Supina, wrote to his draft board in Tucson, Arizona, and said he would not take a physical because "I have absolutely no intention [of aiding] in any way the American war effort against the people of Vietnam."[29]

When men who were drafted refused to report for service, they were jailed. The most famous person to refuse to report for service was heavyweight boxing champion Muhammad Ali. On April 28, 1967, Ali refused to join the army; like many African Americans, he was reluctant to fight a war so that South Vietnamese people could have democratic rights that he felt African Americans in the United States still did not have. Ali said, "I ain't got no quarrel with them Viet Cong [Communist fighters]. No Viet Cong ever called me [derogatory names for black people]."[30] Ali was stripped of his heavyweight title for refusing to join the army, and he was found guilty on June 20, 1967, of the felony charge of draft evasion. The U.S. Supreme Court overturned his charge in 1971, so he did not serve time in jail. However, 3,250 men who refused to be drafted did serve time. In addition, between 40,000 and 125,000 men fled the country to avoid fighting or being jailed.

The Vietnam War revealed huge ideological differences between generations. Many World War I, World War II, and Korean War veterans were offended by the protests. They had been drafted into service and had served without question because they believed it was their duty for their country. Many saw the violence against the protestors as necessary because they were agitators and instigators. Even though the protesters were also only a small fraction of the total population of the country at the time, they were vocal. The Vietnam War was the first time the horror of war was public. Had U.S. news outlets been able to show the devastation of the nuclear bombs in Japan at the end of World War II, there would likely have been large protests against the military much earlier in the country's history. It was not until the Vietnam War that the national evening news listed the number and names of Americans killed each night or that images of body bags, burned and bleeding Vietnamese children, and injured soldiers aired regularly. Protesters saw a direct connection between President Lyndon B. Johnson's authority and the Vietnamese children and teenage American soldiers dying across the ocean.

Soldier Desertion

While thousands of soldiers fled to other countries to avoid the draft, others refused to report for military service when their draft number was called. On June 30, 1966, U.S. Army privates James Johnson, David Samas, and Dennis Mora decided not to go to Vietnam when they got their orders. In a statement, the men, who became known as the Fort Hood Three, said,

We have made our decision. We will not be a part of this unjust,

immoral, and illegal war. We want no part of a war of extermination. We oppose the criminal waste of American lives and resources. We refuse to go to Vietnam!![31]

The three men were court-martialed and sentenced to several years in prison. Many soldiers who fought in Vietnam became convinced the war was wrong, and after their tour of duty was complete, they came home and started Vietnam Veterans Against the War (VVAW), a group dedicated to ending the conflict.

Campuses Erupt

In the summer of 1965, a few hundred people marched in Washington, D.C., against the war. In 1969, however, 500,000 gathered for the Moratorium to End the War in Vietnam. College students were a major force in these anti-war demonstrations. The University of Wisconsin–Madison was one of the most militant anti-war schools, and students clashed repeatedly with police, who used tear gas and physical force to break up the protests. On August 24, 1970, four students detonated a bomb to destroy a research facility the U.S. Army maintained on campus at Sterling Hall.

The bomb did not harm their intended target, but it damaged 26 buildings, killed physicist Robert Fassnacht, and injured 4 other people.

During the 1969 to 1970 academic year, the federal government reported 1,785 student demonstrations, during which students entered and occupied 313 buildings. The most tragic protest was on May 4, 1970, at Kent State in Ohio. When members of the National Guard felt threatened while trying to break up an on-campus protest by several thousand students, they fired into the massed group of students, killing four and wounding nine others.

Four students were killed and nine protesters were injured when Ohio National Guard troops fired into a crowd of people during a demonstration against the Vietnam War on the Kent State University campus.

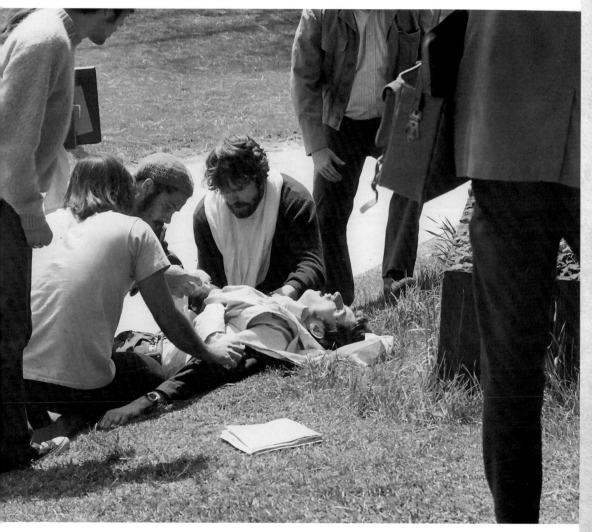

Douglas Wrentmore, a 20-year-old sophomore who was shot in the leg, said,

> The guardsmen, about 50 to 75 of them, had just had a confrontation with the students in the practice football field, and they were marching away. All of a sudden I heard a volley of shots. Girls started screaming. I saw people fall, and I started running and then I fell. I didn't feel anything. One minute I could run and then I could not. Then I saw blood coming from [my] leg.[32]

Student protests over the deaths of Allison Krause, Jeffrey Miller, Sandra Scheuer, and William Knox Schroeder shut down more than 300 campuses in the first and only nationwide strike by U.S. students. More than 4 million students participated in the protests after Kent State's shooting, some of which were violent and included takeovers of hundreds of school buildings. The protests forced many schools to end the spring semester early and skip final examinations.

Other Forms of Protest

In Vietnam, a Buddhist monk burned himself to death to protest the war he believed was hurting his nation. On November 2, 1965, Norman Morrison, a Quaker from Baltimore, Maryland, copied them when he doused himself in kerosene in Washington, D.C., and set himself on fire. Morrison was the first of several Americans who used this extreme form of protest against the war. In addition to these individual acts of protest, the Vietnam War led to the largest and most violent anti-war protests in U.S. history.

This massive opposition by its citizens eventually forced the United States to withdraw from the conflict. The last U.S. soldiers left Vietnam on April 30, 1975, the day after South Vietnam surrendered. It would be more than a quarter century before the nation would again experience such intense anti-war sentiment.

War on Terror

On September 11, 2001, terrorists hijacked four passenger airliners and crashed them into the World Trade Center towers in New York City, the Pentagon in Virginia, and a field in Pennsylvania. Nearly 3,000 people were killed. Because Afghanistan was sheltering the terrorists who planned the act, the United States and several allies invaded it on October 7, 2001. Although there were some protests against the U.S. military actions in Afghanistan, many Americans supported them after the events on September 11.

However, in 2003, when President George W. Bush declared that he wanted to invade Iraq because of their suspected production of weapons of mass destruction, more than 10 million people in 600 cities across the world protested against the invasion. Despite these protests, U.S. forces and a coalition of allies began military action in Iraq on March 20, 2003.

As the fighting in Iraq dragged on and Bush's justifications for the invasion

The Free Speech Movement

The free speech movement began at the University of California, Berkeley, in 1964, and launched Vietnam War protests on campuses. Students had been barred from distributing flyers about political issues. Lynn Hollander Savio, a student active in the free speech movement at the University of California, Berkeley, said that the movement "gave youth in America a sense that political and social action is something that you can and should be involved in and you have power."[1]

1. Quoted in Richard Gonzales, "Berkeley's Fight for Free Speech Fired Up Student Protest Movement," NPR, October 5, 2014. www.npr.org/2014/10/05/353849567/when-political-speech-was-banned-at-berkeley.

Vietnam War demonstrators put flowers into the guns of the police during a protest outside the Pentagon in Arlington, Virginia, in 1967.

proved false, opposition to the war grew rapidly. There were hundreds of mass protests both for and against the war as well as many individual acts of protest

In August 2005, Cindy Sheehan began camping near President Bush's Crawford, Texas, ranch in a protest that drew global media coverage.

such as that of Cindy Sheehan, whose son Casey was killed while fighting on April 4, 2004. Sheehan said, "My son enlisted in the army to protect America and give something back to our country. He didn't enlist to … preemptively attack and occupy a country that was no imminent threat (or any threat) to our country."[33]

As had previously happened during the Vietnam War, soldiers deserted or refused to fight in Iraq. Camilo Mejia, a sergeant in the Florida National Guard, served six months in Iraq but refused to return to duty because he had come to believe that the war was wrong. Mejia was charged with desertion and sentenced to one year in military prison. When he was released from prison, he said, "I was a coward not for leaving the war but for being part of it in the first place."[34]

To mark the sixth anniversary of the invasion of Iraq, thousands of people protested on March 21, 2009. Pat Halle of Baltimore, Maryland, marched for this reason: "We think it's especially important for this new [Obama] administration to feel the pressure from people that we don't want more war."[35] Although the U.S. military presence in Iraq and Afghanistan is not as strong as it was in the early 2000s, people are still speaking out against these military actions.

Chapter Four

WORKERS' RIGHTS

The annual Labor Day picnic in Cincinnati, Ohio, is one of the largest celebrations of Labor Day, the national holiday that honors American workers. The picnic is hosted by the American Federation of Labor and Congress of Industrial Organizations (AFL-CIO), which represents 11 million union workers in every job from miners to nurses and even professional athletes. In a speech at the picnic on September 7, 2009, President Barack Obama reminded a crowd of almost 20,000 people of the many ways in which labor unions have helped make life better for all workers. Obama said,

> We remember that the rights and benefits we enjoy today were not simply handed out to America's working men and women. They had to be won. They had to be fought for, by men and women of courage and conviction [who demanded] an honest day's pay for an honest day's work. Many risked their lives. Some gave their lives. [So] let us never forget: much of what we take for granted—the 40-hour work week, the minimum wage, health insurance, paid leave, pensions [all] bear the union label [and] even if you're not a union member, every American owes something to America's labor movement.[36]

In the more than 100 years since Labor Day became a national holiday, unions have won many important victories for workers, including the standard 8-hour workday, better wages, job security, and better working conditions, sometimes in violent physical confrontations with police, soldiers, and thugs hired by employers. Those clashes resulted in deaths and injuries to workers and even members of their families. This long, bitter fight, which included thousands of protests and riots, has given workers a powerful position in society that early American laborers could not have imagined.

Mother Jones

Once referred to as the most dangerous woman in the United States and one of the most famous women in America in her day, Mary Harris, or Mother Jones, was responsible for hundreds of thousands of workers joining unions. While most women stayed at home and did not join men in acts of protest, Mother Jones kept no permanent address because the labor union cause needed her everywhere in the country. She was one of the orignal signers of the Industrial Workers of the World charter. She included black, female, and child workers in her efforts, a rare move at the time. She even organized the families of workers to support strikes.

She worked heavily with miners, but one of her more memorable roles was leading a march to abolish child labor in 1903, which became front-page news across the nation. She marched with 100 children from the textile mills of Philadelphia, Pennsylvania, all the way to President Theodore Roosevelt's Long Island, New York, home. She was jailed many times, but her actions raised awareness and eventually brought about changes in pay, length of workday, at-work injury and death rates, days off, and the practice of company stores and housing.

Industry Creates Inequality

In 1783, when the colonies defeated Great Britain in the American Revolution, three-fourths of the people residing in the areas that are now New England and the mid-Atlantic states lived and worked on family farms. By 1860, only 40 percent of the men and women in these states still lived and worked on farms, while nearly 1 million people labored in factories in cities. This huge population shift was caused by a growing scarcity of available farmland and the development of machinery and other new technologies that made it possible to mass-produce items such as clothing, shoes, and wheels. These two factors led people in rural areas and new immigrants to flock to big cities to find work in the new industries centered there.

So many people wanted jobs that employers could pay workers substandard wages, fire them for any reason, and make them work long hours under harsh and sometimes dangerous conditions. To gain leverage against their employers, workers banded together in unions in order to bargain with employers as a single unit. Unionizing gave workers the power to shut down operations of the companies by striking, which meant they refused to perform their jobs.

Some of the first workers to strike were women who made shoes and clothing. They were among the most poorly paid workers because companies believed female workers were not worth as much as males. In 1825, the United Tailoresses of New York was the first women's union to strike for higher wages. Then, in Lowell, Massachusetts, in 1834, the Lowell Female Reform Association, made up of women employed in factories weaving cloth, went on strike to protest a wage cut. "Union is power," the striking Lowell workers declared. "Our present object is to have union and exertion, and we remain in possession of our own unquestionable rights."[37] The strike failed, and the Lowell Female Reform Association had to strike several more times through the 1840s before finally winning concessions for better pay and a shorter working day of 10 hours.

A Nation Unites

By 1860, there was a union for nearly every type of job, but their power was somewhat limited because they were localized in cities. However, in July 1877, unions for railroad workers from many cities banded together and staged the most powerful strike up until that time in U.S. history. When Baltimore and Ohio Railroad workers walked off their jobs in West Virginia on July 16, 1877, to protest a 10-percent wage cut, railroad workers throughout several states joined them. Striking workers blocked trains from leaving railroad stations, shutting down rail transportation in a large part of the nation. The anger of the workers also led them to destroy railroad property and battle with police and military units sent to stop them. The August 11, 1877, issue of *Harper's Weekly* magazine described the violence:

Scenes of riot and bloodshed accompanied [the strike] such as we have never before witnessed in the uprising of labor against capital. Commerce has been obstructed, industries have been paralyzed, hundreds of lives sacrificed, and millions of dollars' worth of property destroyed by lawless mobs.[38]

What became known as the Great Railroad Strike of 1877 ended in August when President Rutherford B. Hayes ordered federal troops into Pittsburgh, Pennsylvania, and other cities to stop the violence. It was the first time federal soldiers had been used in a labor dispute. It would not be the last.

The effectiveness of the railroad strike showed workers that a national union could give them more power because it could disrupt the economy on a wider scale. In the late 19th century, the American Federation of Labor (AFL) and Congress of Industrial Organizations (CIO) became major factors in national labor relations. The two groups merged in 1955 to form the American Federation of Labor and Congress of Industrial Organizations (AFL-CIO), the nation's largest combination of unions. These groups and the unions they represented waged a series of violent labor battles in the 20th century to give workers more rights.

Famous Strikes

One of the most violent episodes in U.S. labor history occurred in Ludlow, Colorado, when more than 11,000 coal miners went on strike in September 1913 to protest dangerous working conditions and low wages. After being evicted from company-owned housing, miners and their families lived in a tent city in Ludlow for months while the strike continued. Mine owners convinced state officials to call out the Colorado National Guard because the striking miners were beating replacement workers to keep them away from the mines. On April 20, 1914, there was a violent confrontation between miners and guardsmen. In what became known as the Ludlow Massacre, the guardsmen burned the tent city and fired machine guns into the tents, killing 21 people. (Although some reports list different numbers of casualties.) When miners retaliated by destroying mine property, federal troops were called in to stop them.

Although the strike ended in October with no concessions from the mine owners, the brutal slaying of 66 people, including women and children, made national leaders sympathetic to the plight of workers. In October 1914, Congress passed the Clayton Act, which legalized strikes, boycotts, and picketing by labor groups, and President Woodrow Wilson—who had ordered federal troops to Ludlow—soon signed it into law. Legendary union leader Samuel Gompers hailed the Clayton Act as "the industrial Magna Carta upon which the working people will rear the structure of industrial freedom."[39] Like the Magna Carta, an English document that gave citizens more individual freedom, the Clayton Act gave workers new rights when dealing with their employers.

Violent protests over workers' rights persisted for decades. Historian Paul A. Gilje wrote, "to participants, America appeared on the brink of class warfare."[40] An example of these conflicts occurred between 1936 and 1937 during a sit-down strike at the General Motors (GM) plant in Flint, Michigan. The United Auto Workers (UAW) union, which had been founded in 1935, was trying to negotiate with the automaker for a new contract. GM, like many companies, refused to recognize the union. In protest, workers went on strike but did not leave the plant. Instead, they occupied it, refusing to exit the building. The action became one of history's most famous labor protests.

The Flint sit-down began December 30, 1936, and lasted until February 11, 1937. Family members of the striking workers and members of other unions surrounded the plant to show their support. At times, as many as 10,000 people circled the plant. The supporters also gathered food and other supplies for striking workers. Police tried several times to clear workers from the plant, but strikers used powerful streams of water from fire hoses and threw auto parts to stop police from gaining access to the plant. The resulting loss of production hurt GM so much that it finally agreed to negotiate with the union.

The UAW victory helped to gain wider acceptance for unions in general, which allowed workers in many different types of jobs to win the right to bargain as a collective unit for better wages and working conditions. Harley Shaiken, a University

President Woodrow Wilson, shown here, signed the Clayton Act into law in 1914. The act gave workers more rights.

of California, Berkeley, labor economist, claimed the UAW victory was historically important. He said, "[It] transformed GM, the UAW and much of the economy. That was a pivotal moment in labor history."[41] Shaiken believed that the 1937 UAW victory encouraged millions of other workers to join unions.

Unions are most often associated with urban areas because that is where most union members live. However, people who work on farms also banded together to fight for social and economic changes.

Migrant Workers Fight for Rights

For many decades, farm workers were the largest group of workers unable to form unions to help them bargain with owners of farms on which they worked. Most of these agricultural workers were migrant laborers who traveled from farm to farm to harvest crops such as grapes and lettuce. These workers, many of them Mexican immigrants, had to accept whatever wages and working conditions growers offered them. Owners often ignored labor laws that applied to other workers, such as limiting the number of hours they had to work each day.

This began to change in 1962 when César Chávez and Dolores Huerta began the National Farm Workers Association, which later merged with the Agricultural Workers Organizing Committee in 1966 to become the United Farm Workers (UFW) union. Chávez, a Mexican

Dolores Huerta and César Chávez fought for minimum wages, insurance, and collective bargaining rights, and they even went to work in the fields to recruit farmworkers for their union.

César Chávez (center) made it clear that protests were not truly about products such as grapes or lettuce—at the heart of it, protests were about the people.

The Nation's Largest Employer

America's largest employer, Wal-Mart, employs 2.3 million people, and does not have a union to represent workers' interests. Workers have said that the company pays low wages, and many employees receive federal financial poverty assistance. In the 2000s, major unions organized groups such as Wal-Mart Watch and Wake Up Wal-Mart to promote unionizing. In 2011, the movement began again under the Organization United for Respect at Wal-Mart with the hope that incremental improvements in scheduling, health care, hours, and minimum wage can be made. In 2013, 100 police officers in riot gear arrested more than 50 Wal-Mart workers and supporters during a street protest in Los Angeles, California. Several strikes have been organized, including hunger strikes. The largest strike was in 2014 on Black Friday, the major retail-shopping day after Thanksgiving, and involved 1,600 stores in 49 states.

The movement for a higher minimum wage gained momentum again in 2016. This time, it involved fast food workers striking, as well as Wal-Mart employees, and the protest was for what is called a "living wage."

American, wanted to improve life for farmworkers. Chávez explained,

I had a dream that the only reason the employers were so powerful was not because they in fact had that much power, in terms of dealing with the lives of their workers at will, but what made them truly powerful was that we were weak. And if we could somehow begin to develop some strength among ourselves, I felt that we could begin to equal that, balancing their power in agriculture.[42]

Chávez and Huerta are most famous for organizing a grape boycott to force California grape growers to bargain with the United Farm Workers union so workers would have better working conditions. In 1965, when grape growers would not recognize the union, workers went on strike. To pressure the growers into accepting the union, they began a nationwide campaign to get people to support the union and the boycott by not buying California grapes or products made from California grapes, including wine. The grape boycott was one of the most famous and longest product boycotts in U.S. history, and it was supported by millions of Americans who sympathized with the plight of farm-workers. The boycott lasted five years and forced growers to bargain with the union for higher pay and more benefits.

Workers Make the Nation Stronger

Chávez and Huerta used peaceful tactics in their campaign against grape growers, including several hunger strikes, to gain national attention. Historian Ralph W. Conant explained that "the labor strikes that tore at the fabric of an emerging industrial economy for over half a century are in retrospect interpreted as constructive conflict which was directly responsible for the establishment of the bargaining rights of labor."[43] The right of workers to bargain with employers has helped both them and the nation become economically stronger.

Chapter Five

THE MELTING POT

Racial strife has been a major cause of protests and riots throughout U.S. history. In fact, historians David Boesel and Peter H. Rossi stated,

Of all the sources of civil disorder... none has been more persistent than race. Whether in the North or South, whether before or after the Civil War, whether nineteenth or twentieth century, this question has been at the root of more physical violence than any other.[44]

The group of Americans that has been subjected to racial violence and injustice the longest also was the first to inhabit the land that became the United States—Native Americans. For hundreds of years, war has been waged against Native Americans to take the land from its original inhabitants.

The Wounded Knee Massacre

Wounded Knee is a small community of about 380 people in Oglala Lakota County, South Dakota. It is where two of the most historic events in Native American history took place—the Wounded Knee Massacre in 1890 and the Wounded Knee Occupation nearly a century later in 1973.

On December 23, 1890, 350 men, women, and children of the Lakota band of the Sioux group began a 150-mile (241 km) trek from their village on the Cheyenne River to the Pine Ridge Indian Agency so they could be with other Sioux living there. When they arrived on December 28, 500 soldiers of the Seventh Cavalry forced them to camp at nearby Wounded Knee Creek. Government officials had given the order, fearing the Lakota would join Pine Ridge Sioux in an armed revolt against white settlers in the

There was little media coverage of the occupation at Wounded Knee because the FBI had issued a media blackout to the press. At the 45th Annual Academy Awards in 1973, Marlon Brando sent a Native American activist named Sacheen Littlefeather to decline his award. Littlefeather's speech, while in traditional Apache dress, forced the media to ignore the blackout and report on the occupation.

area. The next day, soldiers disarmed the Lakota and began searching their tents for any remaining weapons. When a shot was heard—no one knows who fired it—the cavalrymen opened fire on the unarmed Sioux with rifles, pistols, and cannons, killing nearly 300 people. American Horse, a Sioux survivor of the massacre, described how soldiers murdered women and children:

The women as they were fleeing with their babes were killed together, shot right through ... After most all of them had been killed a cry was made that all those who were not killed [or] wounded should come forth and they would be safe. Little boys who were not wounded came out of their places of refuge, and as soon as they came in sight a number of soldiers surrounded them and butchered them.[45]

American Indian Movement

The American Indian Movement (AIM) was "founded to turn the attention of Indian people toward a renewal of spirituality which would impart the strength of resolve needed to reverse the ruinous policies of the United States, Canada, and other colonialist governments of Central and South America."[1] AIM has organized many unique, historic protests with the goal of bringing international attention to their causes and bringing change to their conditions. Among their most well-known events are:

- the 19-month occupation of Alcatraz Island in the San Francisco Bay of California in 1969

- the 1970 occupation of a state-controlled dam in Wisconsin that was flooding the Lac Court Orieles Ojibwa reservation

- a 1972 march on Washington, D.C., called the Trail of Broken Treaties, an effort to make the government pay reparations in land and money for the many hundreds of treaties signed and broken

- the 1973 occupation of the historic Wounded Knee Massacre site that resulted in a 71-day face-off against U.S. armed forces and a subsequent trial, which revealed government misconduct

- a 1978 event called the Longest Walk in which Native Americans walked from California to Washington, D.C., to protest laws perceived to discriminate against Native Americans

1. Laura Waterman Wittstock and Elaine J. Salinas, "A Brief History of the American Indian Movement," American Indian Movement, accessed December 12, 2017. www.aimovement.org/ggc/history.html.

Nearly a century after the Wounded Knee Massacre, on the night of February 27, 1973, more than 200 Native Americans drove into Wounded Knee, now a town on the Pine Ridge Reservation, to begin one of the most famous protests in U.S. history. Led by American Indian Movement (AIM) leaders, including

Russell Means, the group occupied the small town for 71 days in an armed stand-off with police, Federal Bureau of Investigation (FBI) agents, and members of the U.S. military. The occupation was staged to make Americans aware of the mistreatment of Native Americans by white people throughout the nation's history and to demand help for their people, who had long struggled since being forced onto reservations. According to Means, the protest was important to Native Americans. He said, "We were about to be obliterated culturally. Our spiritual way of life—our entire way of life was about to be stamped out and this was a rebirth of our dignity and self-pride."[46] The protest ended on May 8 when the Native Americans agreed to peacefully end the occupation.

The massacre and the occupation at Wounded Knee are symbolic of the racist violence that white people have sometimes directed toward Native Americans, African Americans, Asian Americans, and other ethnic groups and the attempts by these groups to fight for the right to be treated as equals.

Demanding Rights

For decades, the action that took place on December 29, 1890, at Wounded Knee Creek was referred to as the Battle of Wounded Knee. Historians now call it the Wounded Knee Massacre because the Lakota had no chance to fight the soldiers that surrounded them. This tragic event was a turning point in American history because it ended a centuries-long war

between white people and Native Americans for control of the United States. Many years before this, the colonists were able to take the Native Americans' land because they had superior arms—rifles, guns, and cannons instead of bows and arrows and spears—and because the many groups scattered across the continent were unable to mount a united front against the newcomers advancing westward from the Atlantic Ocean.

The defeated Native Americans were forced to live on federal reservations where they had little say over how white officials governed their lives. They also were denied basic rights such as voting until June 2, 1924, when Congress finally granted them citizenship. In the 1960s, the African American fight for civil rights inspired Native Americans to start battling the federal government to treat them more fairly.

The new Native American militancy erupted a year later in a dramatic incident on Alcatraz, an island in San Francisco Bay, California, where a famous federal prison once operated. On the morning of November 20, 1969, 89 Native Americans began occupying Alcatraz in a protest that drew worldwide attention. Occupiers claimed the land rightfully belonged to Native Americans. The occupiers held the island until June 11, 1971, when federal officials forcefully removed them. The protest made the nation aware of problems facing Native Americans, such as lack of educational opportunities, high unemployment, and discrimination.

These protests finally convinced the

In 1969, 89 Native Americans occupied the former federal prison on Alcatraz, claiming that the land rightfully belonged to them. They occupied the area until they were forced out by federal officials in 1971.

government to begin treating Native Americans more fairly. In 1970 and 1971, Congress passed 52 legislative proposals to allow Native Americans more power to govern themselves on reservations. The federal government in the 1970s also doubled funds for health care for Native Americans and for money spent on reservations.

The Plight of African Americans

The first Africans arrived in North America in 1619 as indentured servants, but within a few decades, most Africans arriving in the New World were sold as slaves. Although some Africans managed to gain their freedom, most lived in slavery until the end of the Civil War in 1865. In the century following the abolition of slavery, white people in many areas of the nation denied freed black people basic rights and used violence to make them submissive to white rule. This included denying black people due process under the law. White people would often decide on their own that a black person was guilty of a crime and impose a death sentence. Between 1882 and 1968, at least 3,445 black people were lynched, almost all of them in southern states. The term lynch means to kill someone, generally by hanging, as punishment for an alleged offense, but without giving the person a proper and legal trial.

Even though lynchings were brutal, huge crowds sometimes gathered to watch them. On May 21, 1917, a white mob seized Ell Persons, a black man accused of killing a white teenager. *The Memphis Press* later described the mob that watched his death:

> Fifteen thousand of them—men, women, even little children … cheered as they poured the gasoline on [Ell Persons] and struck the match.
>
> They fought and screamed and crowded to get a glimpse of him, and the mob closed in and struggled about the fire as the flames flared high and the smoke rolled about their heads.[47]

Race Riots

White people sometimes attacked black people in race riots. On April 13, 1873, in Colfax, Louisiana, between 60 and 150 black people were beaten or shot to death in a dispute over which political party had won elections the previous November. The massacre began at the Colfax County Courthouse when a white mob murdered black people who had gathered there. White people then went to predominantly black areas of town to beat and kill more black people and burn their homes. Historian Eric Foner called it "the bloodiest single instance of racial carnage in the Reconstruction era."[48]

Reconstruction was the period from the end of the Civil War to 1877 when black Southerners briefly enjoyed rights such as voting because U.S. troops stationed in the South protected them. When the troops left, white southerners took away those rights.

There also were race riots in the early 20th century after black southerners began moving to northern states in large numbers.

Black survivors of the three days of violence in East St. Louis, Illinois, in 1917 called it a race war. It began when hundreds of white workers striking at an aluminum plant saw that black workers were quickly hired to replace them. Violence and emotions ripped through the small town on the river, and soon mobs were pulling black people from streetcars to beat them and even setting the homes of black people on fire to force the occupants outside to be shot. Journalist Carlos F. Hurd reported that it "was a man hunt, conducted on a sporting basis."[49] The town recorded that 39 black people were killed, but others said it was closer to 200. Tulsa, Oklahoma, would later be the site of a race riot in 1921, followed by Rosewood, Florida, in 1923.

Red Summer

Black poet James Weldon Johnson nicknamed the summer of 1919 "Red Summer" because there were more than two dozen race riots in cities including Chicago, Illinois; Philadelphia, Pennsylvania; and New York City. In Chicago on

July 27, a black teenager named Eugene Williams drowned in Lake Michigan after a group of white youths threw rocks at him because he was swimming in an area reserved for white people. Over the next 5 days, at least 23 black people and 15 white people were killed in sporadic fighting, and about 1,000 black people were left homeless when white rioters destroyed their homes. According to a 1922 report on the riot,

Many Negroes were attacked by white ruffians. Streetcar routes, especially at transfer points, were the centers of lawlessness. Trolleys were pulled from the wires, and Negro passengers were dragged into the street, beaten, stabbed, and shot ...

Raids into the Negro residence area then began. Automobiles sped through the streets, the occupants shooting at random. Negroes retaliated by "snip-ing" [shooting guns] from ambush.[50]

For almost a century after slavery ended, African Americans had to endure such violence and were often denied their civil rights. They finally began to win equality with whites and protection under the law through a series of historic protests that lasted more than a decade.

Change Is Going to Come?

African Americans had battled for their rights since slavery was abolished in the late 1800s, but even decades later, they were still discriminated against in every part of the country. Life for black Americans was hardest in the South, where they were forced to endure segregation laws. Black people could not enter businesses reserved for white people, and they had to attend separate schools. They also were denied basic rights, such as voting. Southern laws even forced black people to sit in the rear of buses and to surrender their seat if a white person wanted to sit down. In an act of resistance on December 1, 1955, Rosa Parks, a black woman, refused to give up her seat to a white man on a bus in Montgomery, Alabama. She said later, "We [had] finally reached the point were we [blacks] had to take action."[51] Her personal protest led to her arrest and a year-long boycott of buses by Montgomery's black citizens, which resulted in a U.S. Supreme Court ruling that the Montgomery law was illegal. Similar protests in other southern cities also succeeded in integrating buses so black people could sit anywhere they wanted.

The pace of protests picked up in the 1960s when black Americans battled segregation by staging sit-ins at restaurants that served only whites and by applying to and attending white universities. On September 30, 1962, James Meredith became the first black person admitted to the University of Mississippi. He won the right to attend by filing a federal lawsuit. "My purpose was to break the system of 'White supremacy' at any cost and going to the university was just one of the many steps,"[52] Meredith said. Hundreds of white people came to the

Rosa Parks was a powerful civil rights fighter who was also committed to women's rights. She is shown here after her arrest in 1955 for refusing to give up her bus seat.

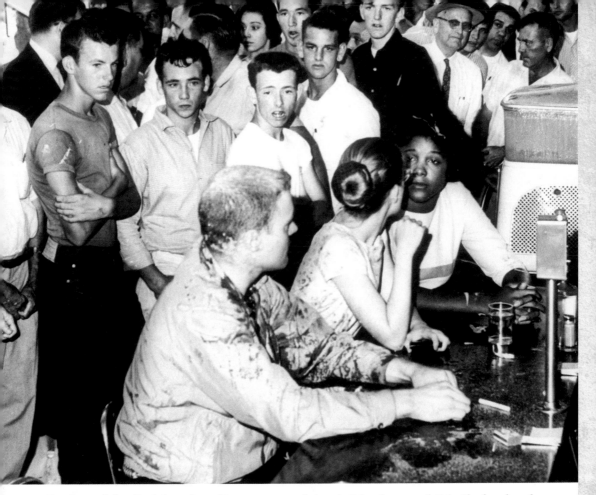

Professor John R. Salter, Joan Trunpauer and Annie Moody, were hit in the head and back and had food poured on them while engaging in a sit-in at a Jackson, Mississippi, restaurant.

campus the day Meredith entered the school to protest his presence. In an armed confrontation with hundreds of federal marshals, 2 civilians were shot to death and 166 federal marshals were injured. Meredith was not harmed and later graduated from the university.

Black Americans staged scores of well-attended marches to defeat segregation. One of the most dramatic was on May 2, 1963, when thousands of children and teenagers marched to the segregated downtown area of Birmingham, Alabama. While they knelt and prayed, police arrested 959 of them for parading without a permit—white officials had refused them permission for the march. When 15-year-old Grosbeck Preer Parham appeared in court, a white judge warned him that black people should stop protesting. The judge advised him that black people should be patient and they would eventually get their rights. The teenager replied, "We've been waiting

March on Washington for Jobs and Freedom

On August 28, 1963, 250,000 people gathered near the Lincoln Memorial in Washington, D.C., in perhaps the single most important civil rights protest in history. The March on Washington for Jobs and Freedom is best remembered for the "I Have a Dream" speech given by Martin Luther King Jr., but veteran civil rights leader Ralph Abernathy believed the protest's true importance was the impact of so many people gathering together on a single day to support African American civil rights:

> The March on Washington established visibility in this nation. It showed the struggle [for black rights] was nearing a close, that people were coming together, that all the organizations could stand together. It demonstrated that there was a unity in the black community for the cause of freedom and justice. It made it clear that we did not have to use violence to achieve the goals which we were seeking.[1]

1. Quoted in Henry Hampton and Steve Fayer, *Voices of Freedom: An Oral History of the Civil Rights Movement from the 1950s Through the 1980s.* New York, NY: Bantam, 1990, pp. 169–170.

over one hundred years."[53]

The protests of the 1960s ended the injustice of segregation laws by forcing the federal government to intervene and make southern states grant black citizens full and equal rights. Christopher Wilson of the National Museum of American History explained how the change of the civil rights movement worked:

> Many things were happening all at once—connecting, conflicting, building, diverting from one another all at the same time. When we look, we remember back at all of the [civil rights] Movement's pieces and moments as leading to the ultimate legal victories ... but the truth is there wasn't one, there were many and they were often competitive ... It took boycotts, petitions, news coverage, civil disobedience, marches, lawsuits, shrewd political maneuvering, fundraising, and even the violent terror campaign of the movement's opponents—all going on in the same time.[54]

Although the civil rights movement led to many significant victories, black people have continued to protest into the 21st century to achieve true equality with white people.

Mobs and Lynchings

In the early days of the American West, before California was even a state, racial prejudice was rampant. Chinese people had come over in two major waves during the beginning of the Gold Rush in 1849 and as laborers for the first transcontinental railroad. They were subjected to laws and punishing taxes written specifically against their race. There were no courts to handle accusations or problems in the days before California's statehood in 1850, and most attempts at justice were served by white lynch mobs.

Some white Americans, and even some Mexican Americans, feared that Chinese gold-seekers would steal from them or take their jobs by being willing to work for less money, so violent attacks on Chinese camps and individuals were frequent and deadly. In 1884, an Irish railroad worker was freed after killing a Chinese man because the judge could find no law protecting Chinese people living in America from murder. When the Gold Rush was over and the railroad was built, Chinatowns in several cities became home for these Chinese workers. Discriminatory laws limited opportunities to work, live, and marry. They could not educate their children in public schools or testify in court, even as the victim of an attack. The only way to survive was to form tight-knit communities. Anti-Chinese organizations followed wherever Chinatowns were established.

Internment

Japanese immigrants also faced racist attacks. In the 1940s, when the United States began fighting Japan in World War II, the U.S. government forcibly interned 120,000 Japanese American men, women, and children in 10 camps. These Japanese Americans were imprisoned in the camps for up to three years because the government believed they might sabotage the war effort against their former homeland.

Racism against Asian Americans resurged in the 1980s when Japanese automakers began selling more cars than U.S. automakers, which resulted in some U.S. workers losing their jobs. On June 19, 1982, Vincent Chin, a Chinese American, was beaten to death with a baseball bat in Detroit, Michigan, by Ronald Ebens and Michael Nitz, who mistakenly believed Chin was Japanese. When the attackers received only three years of probation and a fine, Asian Americans formed the American Citizens for Justice. The group staged protests, demanded a retrial, and asked the federal government to investigate whether Chin's civil rights had been violated. Two decades later in a ceremony remembering Chin's death, Elaine Akagi, who worked with the Organization of Chinese Americans to seek justice for his death, said, "As tragic as [his] death was, one good thing was that it banded Asian Americans together. If nothing else, we started working together on issues, not only Vincent's death."[55]

The Chicano Movement

Mexican Americans also organized their own movements. The first Mexican Americans lived in California and parts of the Southwest before the United States won the territory from Mexico in the 1840s. Mexican Americans and other Latinx people experienced discrimination from white Americans in both the 19th and 20th centuries. The Mexican Americans in the Southwest called their cause the Chicano Movement. Many Mexicans had become Americans at the end of the Mexican-American War in 1848, but discrimination, education segregation, police harassment, and limited voting rights separated them from whites. Workers' rights, especially farm workers' rights, were also a major part of the movement through the activism of César Chávez and Dolores Huerta, although their work went beyond Mexican Americans.

High school students were an important and visible part of the movement as well. They organized walkouts from schools in Denver, Colorado, and Los Angeles in 1968 to protest bans on speaking Spanish and the high dropout rates among Chicano high school students. A militant youth group called the Brown Berets was formed as a response to the police brutality that Mexican Americans faced in Los Angeles and was modeled after the Black Panther party. In 1972, the Brown Berets occupied Catalina Island off the coast of Los Angeles to protest the United States' illegal seizure and occupation of their indigenous lands. The group still exists today, protesting and organizing on behalf of their community.

Immigration Protests

Mexican Americans also fought for the rights of both documented and undocumented immigrants—they wanted it to be easier for other people to come to the United States and for the nation to treat undocumented immigrants with more fairness.

On May 1, 2006, millions of Latinx people staged a "Day without Immigrants" in which they refused to go to school, to work, or to shop at any stores. So many workers participated in the protest that some restaurants and other businesses had to close. In Los Angeles, 500,000 protesters wore white shirts and chanted things César Chávez had said. In Chicago, 400,000 protesters gathered, and 75,000 protested in Denver. Demonstrations occurred in more than 140 cities in 39 states. Signs such as "Am I Not a Human Being?" were carried in marches. Overall, an estimated 1.1 million Latinx people marched.

In 2017, the "Day without Immigrants" was again used to protest harsh treatment and to remind Americans what an economy without immigrant labor and buyers would look like. Both events highlighted the fact that immigrant workers make up a significant portion of the American workforce.

Dreamers Deferred

In June 2012, activists organized hunger strikes and sit-ins in Obama's reelection campaign offices to push for protections for immigrants. This and other pressures resulted in Obama starting the Deferred Action for Childhood Arrivals (DACA) program later that month to protect and support immigrants who had been brought into the United States as children and not documented. Since they were too young when the act happened to be held responsible, DACA argued, they should be allowed to get work permits and go to college. More than 800,000 undocumented immigrants, nicknamed "Dreamers," have been helped through the program as of 2017. However, plans to potentially end DACA were proposed in 2017. This was widely protested. Hundreds of students walked out of Denver schools to protest in support of students who were undocumented immigrants.

Islamophobia

After September 11, 2001, a new form of intolerance began to rise in the United States. Violence was perpetrated

In 2017, a group of 15 teenage girls stood in front of the Texas State Capitol in quinceañera *dresses as a public protest against Texas' SB4 bill, which was called the "sanctuary cities bill." Called "Quinceañera at the Capitol," around 250 people showed up to rally with the teenagers on the steps of the Texas capitol building.*

across America, not only against innocent Muslims and their mosques but also against Sikhs, Indians, and anyone else who uninformed people perceived to be from the Middle East. Major protests erupted against a proposal to build a community center near the site of the 2001 attacks in lower Manhattan because the center would include a mosque and be run by American Society for Muslim Advancement and the Cordoba Initiative, a group that represents Muslims in the Western world.

From college students leading marches against Islamophobia to protesters organizing against new mosques and Muslim community centers, the protests, and sometimes the violence, has persisted years after the attacks. Donald Trump's 2017 proposed travel restrictions against a number of predominantly Muslim countries led to more protests against Islamophobia and policies that are unfair to Muslims.

Chapter Six

A STRUGGLE THROUGHOUT HISTORY

The world's first women's rights convention was held in 1848 in Seneca Falls, New York, when more than 300 women and men met on July 19 and 20 to debate and approve a "Declaration of Sentiments and Resolutions." This document called for an end to gender discrimination against women and laid out the goals of the women's rights movement, from winning the right to vote to gaining legal equality with men. Patterned after the Declaration of Independence, the declaration stated,

> We hold these truths to be self-evident: that all men and women are created equal; that they are endowed by their Creator with certain inalienable rights; that among these are life, liberty, and the pursuit of happiness; that to secure these rights governments are instituted, deriving their just powers from the consent of the governed.[56]

Voting Is Power

Women realized the key to achieving equality with men was winning the right to vote. This would enable them to elect officials who supported them. The fight for women's suffrage, or the right to vote, took seven decades to achieve. Women and their male supporters held political rallies, signed petitions, and engaged in acts of civil disobedience to win the right to vote. Lucy Stone of Massachusetts refused to pay taxes because she could not vote. To get payment for the taxes she owed, government officials seized Stone's household goods, including her baby's cradle.

In 1869, Stone founded the American Woman Suffrage Association, which became the most influential of several groups working for women's suffrage. In 1869, the territorial legislature of Wyoming granted women the right to vote. In 1890, when Wyoming became a state,

From January 1917 until June 1919, women picketed in front of the White House to protest the federal government's refusal to allow women to vote. The women became known as Silent Sentinels because they marched peacefully and quietly while carrying protest signs.

it was the first state to grant women the right to vote, and others eventually followed. It was harder to convince the federal government to grant this right because it required a change to the U.S. Constitution. In 1878, a constitutional amendment to allow women to vote was introduced for the first time. Congress, however, rejected it repeatedly over the next four decades.

In 1917, Alice Paul created the National Woman's Party (NWP) for women's suffrage. On January 10, 1917, a dozen NWP members began picketing the White House to persuade President Woodrow Wilson to support suffrage. On June 22, police arrested two female picketers on a charge of obstructing traffic because cars were stopping to watch them. Police arrested more women in the next few months, including Paul on October 20. Many protesters were beaten and treated abusively in jail, and Paul was one of several women brutally force-fed with tubes during a hunger strike in protest of their arrest. The women protesters, known as Silent Sentinels, continued picketing daily until Congress approved the 19th Amendment to the Constitution.

The Force Reawakens

Women made progress in many areas in the decades after they won the right to vote. They could enroll in college and engage in political activity. World War I and World War II had proved that women could work in factories, contribute to the economy, and continue raising children. After World War II especially, many women were reluctant to return to their previous lives. However, in the 1960s, women were still not treated equally in many areas, including the workplace. They were still denied certain jobs and paid less than men. Women again protested, demanding equality.

On the final night of the 1968 Miss America Pageant, nearly 400 people were assembled to protest the pageant. As television cameras recorded live, protesters dropped a banner over a balcony railing that read, "Women's Liberation," and the second wave of feminism received its first instance of national attention. Their fight became known as the women's liberation movement, and its goal was to achieve legal and social equality with men. The movement provided many new opportunities for women in the workplace, sports,

and politics, as female candidates were elected to many levels of government.

However, repeated attempts by women's groups to pass an Equal Rights Amendment to the U.S. Constitution that would bar any discrimination based on biological sex has failed for decades. The proposed amendment states that the Constitution applies equally to all persons regardless of their biological sex. It passed through Congress in 1972, but it was not ratified by the states within an extended 10-year time limit. Since 1983, the act has been reintroduced during every congressional session.

Abortion Debate

Women also have waged a bitter fight over abortion for more than four decades. Before the 1970s, many states banned abortion services, which forced thousands of women to get abortions illegally. Many women believed they should have complete control over their own body and reproductive choices, and they began working to repeal laws limiting abortion access by challenging the laws in court. On January 22, 1973, U.S. Supreme Court case *Roe v. Wade* overturned a Texas law restricting access to abortion services and allowed women to terminate a pregnancy within the first three months after conception—after three months, states could regulate abortion. The ruling legalized abortion services throughout the United States and was considered a major triumph for women's rights, but people who opposed granting women the right to terminate a pregnancy began fighting

People have protested against abortion for decades. One protest that occurs every October is the Life Chain protest, in which people against abortion line up along stretches of highways holding pro-life signs.

immediately to once again limit access to abortion services or make abortion procedures illegal. This fierce battle has played a major role in national politics ever since.

Pro-choice activists continue to engage in many protests to publicize the issue. One of the most massive was the April 24, 2004, March for Women's Lives, when more than 1 million people held a rally in Washington, D.C. Anti-abortion, or pro-life, supporters also have engaged in dramatic protests to publicize their political point of view. One common tactic they have used is to picket outside medical offices where abortion services are provided to intimidate pregnant women and the medical practitioners who provide abortion services.

Demanding LGBT+ Rights

Some pro-life supporters advocate for adoption as an alternative to abortion, but some people also have strong opinions about who should or should not have the

Lack of Concern About AIDS

AIDS became a worldwide epidemic beginning in the early 1980s. The U.S. government was slow to fund research into treatment protocols for AIDS because gay men were the group hit hardest in the early days of the disease. Before AIDS had a formal name, it was even referred to by some people as "gay cancer." In 1987, the AIDS Coalition to Unleash Power (ACT UP) was created to protest the lack of concern over AIDS. ACT UP staged many dramatic protests to attract media coverage about the need for more funding. On September 14, 1989, seven ACT UP members invaded the New York Stock Exchange and chained themselves to a balcony to protest the high price of AIDS drugs. In December 1989, approximately 4,500 people protested at New York's St. Patrick's Cathedral, one of many protests held at churches whose denominations condemned homosexuality. One of the most daring acts of protest occurred on January 22, 1991, when three ACT UP members entered the studio of the CBS Evening News at the beginning of the nationally televised broadcast. Anchorman Dan Rather had just introduced himself when the ACT UP members shouted for AIDS to be fought, not wars. Microphones picked up the protesters' voices, and Rather cut immediately to a commercial break.

As of 2016, 36.7 million people worldwide were living with HIV/AIDS, including 2.1 million children, and an estimated 35 million people have died from AIDS-related illnesses.

ACT UP activists marched in 1994 on the 25th anniversary of the Stonewall riots.

right to adopt and raise children. Some believe that only married couples should be allowed to have children, and that marriage is only right when it is between a man and a woman. Many also hold the belief that sexual orientation is a choice.

For decades, being gay was considered a psychiatric condition. For hundreds of years, sexual contact between anyone but a man and a woman could potentially lead to forced institutionalization, sterilization, imprisonment, banishment, and even death. Even as late as the 1960s, many states still had laws that prohibited sexual contact between members of the same sex.

On January 1, 1967, police beat and arrested more than a dozen people at the Black Cat Bar in Los Angeles for kissing each other because they were of the same sex. They were kissing to celebrate the new year, a traditional way for many people to greet the new year, but because many of the partygoers identified as gay, the tradition was technically illegal. These arrests sparked protests. An editorial in *The Advocate*, an LGBT+ news publication, predicted that LGBT+ people would no longer passively allow police or anyone else to deny them their rights. The newspaper boldly declared, "We do not ask for our rights on bended knee. We demand them, standing tall, as dignified human beings. We will not go away."[57]

Stonewall

The prophecy declared by *The Advocate* in 1967 came true with the riots at the Stonewall Inn in New York City in 1969. Police at that time regularly raided such bars and harassed gay men, sometimes arresting them for even minor acts of public contact, such as kissing, which was still illegal at the time. That night, however, customers at the Stonewall resisted arrest. When police began to arrest the bar's patrons, a crowd gathered outside the bar and soon joined the Stonewall customers in fighting police. Outnumbered and fearing for their safety, police retreated from the bar. The event set the stage for national protests. By openly fighting police, the Stonewall riots helped bring the plight of LGBT+ people to the attention of the public and emboldened many LGBT+ people elsewhere to stand up for equal rights. Protests continued, resulting in more than 200,000 people protesting at the National March on Washington for Lesbian and Gay Rights on October 14, 1979. Lesbian photographer and filmmaker Joan E. Biren said of the march:

> *You were just amazed and astounded to see so many of our own people in one place. I was very publicly out, but there were not too many others who were. The triumph of the 1979 march was that so many people did come out. To me, the importance was we were going to be a political force. This was the most visible we had ever been.*[58]

The mass gathering was similar to smaller "pride" parades and festivals

The White Night Riots

San Francisco, California, was nicknamed "the Gay Capital of America," and has a popular, politically engaged gay district called the Castro. When former government worker Dan White was given only seven years in prison in 1979 for the murder of the first openly gay elected official in the country, City Supervisor Harvey Milk, and Mayor George Moscone, the Castro erupted. Protesters poured onto the streets and began marching, blocking traffic as hundreds became 5,000.

By the time they reached the city's civic center, anger erupted. Windows and doors were smashed, and a fire was started inside the building. City Hall was trashed. Hundreds of police showed up in riot gear, but they were ordered not to engage with the mob. A dozen police cars were set on fire, and the police were finally given orders to suppress the crowd. After being tear-gassed, the mob retreated back to the Castro, but the police soon followed seeking retaliation.

Removing their badges and names, the police rioted and even destroyed a gay bar, called the Elephant Walk. After an FBI investigation, the police riot was determined to have been highly illegal, and the city paid millions in restitution to victims of the violence. The next night, San Francisco's gay community and its supporters held an event in honor of Harvey Milk on Castro Street to show that the police violence did not crush their spirit. More than 20,000 people showed up.

Many of the protesters during the what was known as the white night riots fought back against the police with tree branches, street signs, parking meters, and rocks.

already being held in cities throughout the nation. The Stonewall riots were commemorated every June thereafter through pride marches held in many cities. Another march in the nation's capital on October 11, 1987, drew more than 200,000 people, and another march in 1993 drew more than 800,000.

In the decades after the Stonewall riots, the fight for gay rights has won legal protections against job discrimination, state and federal hate crime laws, the repeal of laws that criminalize intercourse between people of the same biological sex, and more funding for research and treatment for HIV/AIDS.

The Military Ban

In 1981, the Department of Defense (DoD) issued a ban on LGBT+ people serving openly in the military, stating that homosexuality was not compatible with military service. The ban was reissued in 1982, 1993, and 2008, despite that fact that reports commissioned by the DoD concluded that homosexuals posed no significant security risk. When Bill Clinton campaigned for the presidency in 1992, he promised to overturn the ban on homosexuality in the military, but after failing to overcome opposition, he compromised by signing the policy known as "Don't Ask, Don't Tell" (DADT) into law in 1993.

With more than 13,000 people discharged using DADT, it became clear that the compromise was not a compromise at all. In 2007, Barack Obama campaigned for the presidency and promised to repeal the controversial policy within the first 100 days after taking office. In 2010, 13 gay military rights activists handcuffed themselves to the White House fence. As they were cut off the fence and carried into police custody to be arrested and jailed, they chanted that they wanted to serve and wanted equality and visibility. It took another DoD report and many protests for President Obama to finally make good on his promise in 2010.

In June 2016, Obama lifted the military ban on transgender service members, but it was reinstated by President Trump in 2017. In response, New York City's Times Square was flooded with hundreds of protesters, and "emergency" marches were held in San Francisco; Portland, Oregon; Washington, D.C.; and Los Angeles. Later in 2017, the proposed reinstatement of the ban was put on hold, paving the way for transgender people to enlist in the military once again.

Marriage Rights

Another battle gay and lesbian people still were fighting in the 21st century was for the right to legally marry their same-sex partners. Gay and lesbian couples wanted to show their love for each other by marrying and receiving all the legal rights married couples have, such as spousal workplace benefits and being able to jointly own property. Thousands of marches, rallies, and other protests were held by both sides in the battle over same-sex marriage. Ultimately, the right

The passage of Proposition 8, which made same-sex marriage illegal in California, stunned gay and lesbian couples throughout California, who truly believed the fight for the right to marry was already over in their state. Many people in the state marched in support of LGBT+ rights at this time.

to marry was granted in 2015 by the U.S. Supreme Court.

The Transgender Rights Movement

The transgender rights movement pulls together issues of gay rights, women's rights, and the rights of minorities. Although transgender people were frequently active participants in LGBT+ events, such the Stonewall riots, pride parades, and marches on Washington, D.C., the community has recently formed their own movement specific to the concerns and needs that they feel were sometimes ignored by members of the communities they protested with. It was only in 2016, for example, that transgender people were allowed to openly serve in the military—and that policy is still being challenged. Four decades after homosexuality was removed from the list of

A 2017 rally to support transgender and gender nonconforming students took place in New York City outside the Stonewall Inn, which has become the site of many protests throughout American history.

mental illnesses, transgender people finally saw that change for themselves in 2012. It took until 1993 for any state to ban discrimination against transgender people, although people who identify as gay or lesbian had their first state success against discrimination in 1982.

In 2016 and 2017, protests erupted over access to bathrooms. North Carolina passed a law stating that public school and public agency bathroom access must be restricted to the sex on one's birth certificate, invalidating the identity of transgender people. In response, hundreds of protesters gathered at the Stonewall Inn, and dozens of protesters were arrested at a protest at the North Carolina state house. Several hundred people gathered outside the White House to protest, chanting that transgender students were welcome there and there was not hate or fear of them. More than 150,000 people signed

Intersectionality

In 2017, there was a growing movement within the LGBT+ community to act in solidarity with people outside of their community. People who have in the past only protested for their own causes have gathered and protested in a show of support for other groups that are not treated equally in recognition of the struggle they all have in common. The LGBT+ community rallied by the thousands at Stonewall Inn to support the rights of immigrants, protesting the Trump administration's 2017 travel restrictions placed against people from predominantly Muslim countries and the rescindment of DACA. LGBT+ groups have also responded to the Black Lives Matter movement, sharing a common understanding of murders in their communities being marginalized. The solidarity movement has been referred to as "intersectionality" to recognize the intersections of race, class, gender, and sexual identity issues.

a petition demanding repeal of the North Carolina ruling.

Rallies have also been held to respond to the brutal violence that many transgender people have faced. The National Day of Action to End Violence Against Transgender Women of Color organized events in many cities to protest increasing violence that has led to the murder of more than 55 transgender people, the majority of whom were women of color, between January 2015 and March 2017.

Making History by Fighting for One's Rights

Women and other minorities who have fought for their rights have often had to do things that outraged other people, such as picketing at the White House to gain the right to vote. By doing so, they made history. Historian Laurel Thatcher Ulrich wrote that, "Well-behaved women seldom make history."[59] Ulrich's comment can be said of every group that has taken a stand for their rights.

HISTORY REPEATING

Historian Richard C. Wade wrote: "Violence is no stranger to American cities. [For] two centuries, American cities have known the physical clash of groups, wide-scale breakdown of established authority, and bloody disorder."[60] It is natural that so much disorder and violence has occurred in cities because many different types of people live in close proximity to one another. This closeness has often allowed differences between various groups of race, nationality, language, or religion to erupt into violence.

Early Riots

During the winter months of 1734, poor people in Exeter, New Hampshire, illegally chopped down trees owned by wealthy people so they could burn the wood to keep warm. When British officials sent Daniel Dunbar and a group of armed men to Exeter on April 23 to arrest the thieves, local citizens banded together to stop them. An official wrote, "A great number of ill-disposed persons assembled themselves [and] in a riotous, tumultuous and most violent manner did beat wound and terribly abuse a number of men."[61]

Hunger caused the flour riot in New York City on February 10, 1837. When flour merchants hoarded flour to force its price to rise, angry citizens broke into warehouses where the flour was stored and stole it. There were also riots over food in the South when fighting during the Civil War caused food shortages and boosted the prices of food. On April 17, 1864, a group of 50 to 100 women descended on local stores in Georgia and demanded that the owners sell them bread at a fair price. When the owners did not respond quickly enough, the women took the bread without paying for it. Three women were arrested, but officials did not want to punish people who could not

Protests at Charlottesville

A rmed white nationalists and neo-Nazis fought counter protesters in Charlottesville, Virginia, in August 2017 during a march called Unite the Right. It became one of the most violent white nationalist protests in recent decades. Thousands of people participated in the demonstration, and a man drove his car into the counter protesters, killing one and injuring nineteen.

In October 2017, they returned with a rally called "Charlottesville 3.0." Both events were protests against the city removing a statue of Confederate General Robert E. Lee from a city park as part of a national movement to remove Confederate flags and statues from public and government properties and to rename buildings at Southern public schools and universities.

afford to buy food. An article published in *The News* said, "That the present high prices of provisions have provided distress no one can doubt, and it is probably that some who participated in the riotous proceedings of yesterday were goaded to their course by pressure of want."[62]

Immigrants

Discrimination also often led to physical confrontations and riots between immigrants and Americans who rejected them. One expert said, "Violent social conflict in America has generally occurred when the established order resisted efforts of new or excluded groups to gain access to rights and opportunities ostensibly available to [everyone]."[63]

In 1855 in Louisville, Kentucky, some were worried that the growing number of German immigrants would influence the August 6 election. A political party that opposed immigrants and Catholic people tried to stop Germans from voting. They gathered at voting locations and beat and even killed German immigrants who were there to cast a ballot. When the Germans defended themselves, a gun battle and riot began. Although many historians claim that 22 people died in what became known as Bloody Monday, some estimates of the dead range as high as 100.

On February 21, 1909, in Omaha, Nebraska, between 500 and 1,000 people gathered to discuss an incident that had occurred two days earlier in which a Greek immigrant shot and killed a police officer who tried to arrest him. At the gathering, attorney H. C. Murphy claimed that Greeks were undesirable neighbors. He said, "The blood of an American is on the hands of these Greeks and some method should be adopted to avenge his death and rid the city of this class of persons."[64] The men then rushed into the street toward Greek Town, collecting more participants along the way before they began rioting. Eventually, more than 3,000 men and boys destroyed 30 buildings and burned and looted Greek businesses and homes. The mob beat men, women, and children, and one boy was killed.

A Nation on Fire

In 1964, several cities, most notably New York City; Rochester; and Philadelphia, Pennsylvania, exploded in riots. In August 1965, the Watts neighborhood of Los Angeles was triggered into riot. In 1966, 43 riots occurred. By 1967, riots were even hitting smaller cities, although the worst were in Newark, New Jersey, and Detroit, Michigan. In Newark, the National Guard shot into occupied public housing. Some people believe that Detroit never recovered.

Many of these events were triggered by brutal police altercations with African Americans that quickly erupted into citywide violence as word of the injustice spread. The 1964 New York riots began in response to a white police officer shooting a black teenager named James Powell. The 1964 Rochester event began after a 19-year-old was arrested for public intoxication at a block party. The 1965 Watts riots began with a traffic stop that spiraled into violence. The 1967 Newark riots began after police severely beat a black cab driver during a traffic stop and ended with 26 dead. People in Detroit rioted for five days after the police raided an illegal, after-hours nightclub whose patrons were mostly African Americans.

Then, Martin Luther King Jr. was assassinated on April 4, 1968, and over the next week, riots broke out in 125 cities. In Chicago, Illinois, and Baltimore, Maryland, tens of thousands of soldiers were sent in to suppress the violence. Machine guns were mounted on the steps of the U.S. Capitol Building. Many black Americans were enraged, and many whites were terrified by the anger. When the Holy Week Uprising's fires finally died, 39 people had been killed, more than 2,600 were injured, and 21,000 people had been arrested.

The Response

After the Newark and Detroit riots of 1967, President Lyndon B. Johnson called for a national investigation into the previous years of violent upheavals. The Kerner Commission uncovered that police altercations were the catalyst for half of the 24 riots it studied. It also uncovered a truth that shocked white politicians: None of these riots were the result of outside agitators or militant groups, as they had assumed. Instead the commission reported:

White racism is essentially responsible for the explosive situation, which has been accumulating in our cities since the end of World War II. Pervasive discrimination and segregation in

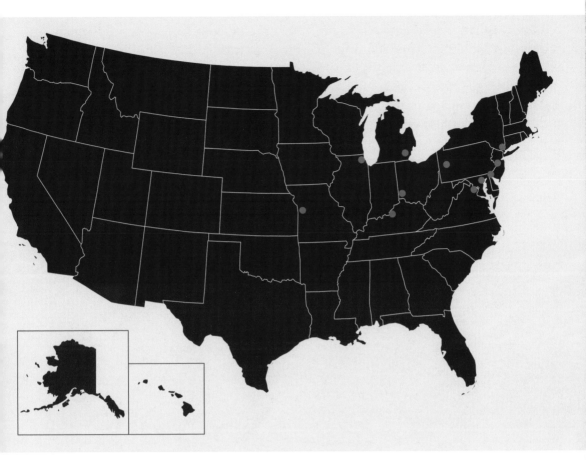

The Holy Week Uprising after King's assassination resulted in more than $65 million in damages to public and private property across major U.S. cities. Locations where major riots occurred are highlighted with circles.

employment, education and housing have resulted in the continuing exclusion of great numbers of Negroes from the benefits of economic progress.[65]

It also predicted that other, worse events were to come. It was, sadly, correct: King's assassination occurred a month after the report was turned in. A follow-up report, titled "One Year Later," said that the government's response to the riots "has been perilously inadequate.

The nation has merely come one year closer to being 'two societies, one black and one white, separate and unequal.'"[66]

The Kerner Commission was not, however, without a solution. It proposed a massive public-works program with 2 million jobs, a basic minimum income for urban families, and the building of 6 million new units of affordable housing. These were radical changes, and no one in Washington, D.C., was ready to shift such a significant sum of money to black causes or even hear, let alone accept, that racism was an issue. The commission was instead ignored; President Johnson even refused to formally receive it. Richard Nixon was elected president a short time later. One of his election promises was a "war on crime" through strict law and order. He fulfilled his promise soon after being elected by funding police departments with body armor, tear gas, and tanks. Funding cuts in housing, schools, and job training would continue for decades. The decisions of Presidents Johnson and Nixon would reset the cycle of violence. Countless incidents where black people were beaten, unlawfully arrested and imprisoned, and even killed by police followed, and more riots occurred.

One of American's next major periods of racial tension followed the 1991 assault of Rodney King, a black man, by four

The whole world saw the kicking, bashing, and beating of a black man by white police, and when it was announced that the officers who assaulted Rodney King were not guilty, Los Angeles residents rioted in places such as this grocery store.

police officers in Los Angeles. A doctor who treated King after the beating said that "some bones were so pulverized they were like grains of sand."[67] Rodney King said that he felt lucky to be alive.

Someone had filmed the horrific beating from their home and gave the film to the local news. However, the police officers were found not guilty, and Los Angeles erupted in riots in 1992 that lasted five days. In the aftermath of the verdict and the riots that followed, 63 people were dead, more than 12,000 were arrested, close to 3,000 were injured, and $1 billion dollars in damage had been done to the city.

The Cycle Continues

Journalist Deborah Small wrote, "Every big city had a black ghetto and every black ghetto had for decades been experiencing the same grievances: hatred and mistrust of police, unending poverty, discrimination, despair, alienation and increasing frustration with white resistance to nonviolent appeals for justice."[68] She was referring to the riots of the 1960s, but could just as easily have been writing about the causes of the Black Lives Matter movement.

In 2013, a jury found George Zimmerman not guilty of the 2012 shooting of 17-year-old Trayvon Martin. Both the shooting and the jury's decision sparked protests in more than 100 cities. President Barack Obama explained, "It's important to recognize that the African-American community is looking at this issue through a set of experiences and a history

that doesn't go away."[69]

In July 2014, Eric Garner, a black man in Staten Island, New York, was killed after being placed in a chokehold by white officers during an arrest for being suspected of illegally selling loose cigarettes. A month later, Michael Brown, an unarmed black teenager was killed, this time by a white police officer in Ferguson, Missouri. Protests shook the city for weeks, and when the grand jury decided not to indict the officer, Ferguson responded with rioting. Protests after both the murder and grand jury verdict also occurred across the country. Rioter Brien Redmon said, "This is not about vandalizing ... This is about fighting a police organization that doesn't care about the lives they serve."[70] President Obama responded to the rioting by saying, "We have made enormous progress in race relations over the course of the past several decades ... but what is also true is that there are still problems, and communities of color aren't just making these problems up."[71] A federal investigation of the Ferguson Police Department revealed that they had engaged in so many constitutional violations that they needed to be completely retrained, echoing the complaints that many in Ferguson had made for years.

Tamir Rice, a black 12-year-old boy in Cleveland, Ohio, was also shot by white police in 2014. In 2015, Baltimore was rocked by weeks of protests and riots after the death of 25-year-old Freddie Gray from a spinal cord injury after suspected police abuse at the time of his arrest for suspected weapons possession. It was later shown that Gray was not carrying a weapon at the time of his arrest. Once again, the country was reminded of the systemic injustices black Americans have suffered for decades.

In 2016, Philando Castile, a legally armed 32-year-old black man, was pulled over for a broken tail light and soon thereafter shot and killed by a St. Paul, Minnesota, police officer. Castile was killed in front of his girlfriend and four-year-old daughter. Later in 2016, Alton Sterling, a 37-year old black man, was shot at close range while being held to the ground by white police officers in Baton Rouge, Louisiana. In 2017, a jury acquitted the police officer who killed Sterling, and protests followed throughout the city.

In a high-profile protest against acts of police brutality and racism, Colin Kaepernick, an NFL quarterback, publicly protested by kneeling as "The Star-Spangled Banner" played before games during the 2016 to 2017 football season.

As an act of protest against police brutality, Colin Kaepernick (center) kneeled during the national anthem at the start of each football game.

What's in a Name?

Newspapers and historians record these violent black events as riots, but some participants disagree. Some see these violent events as rebellions or uprisings. Some people might shake their heads and call the violence senseless, but again, participants disagree. "People participate in this type of event for a real reason," said UCLA professor Darnell Hunt. "It's not just anger and frustration at the immediate or proximate cause. It's always some underlying issues."[1] Lonnie Bunch, director of the National Museum of African American History and Culture, argued the same point:

> I think what's really clear is that there's a lack of knowledge about everything from what does urban unrest mean, to what does it tell you historically about people who burn and destroy in their own neighborhoods, to really the way people are characterized? And so in some ways as I watch the media coverage of Baltimore, Ferguson and other things, I'm amazed at how ahistorical the coverage is.
>
> How people do not understand that in some ways this is part of a long tradition where people who feel devalued find ways to find a voice.[2]

1. Quoted in German Lopez, "Riots are Destructive, Dangerous, and Scary—But can Lead to Serious Social Reforms," Vox, September 22, 2016. www.vox.com/2015/4/30/8518681/protests-riots-work.

2. Quoted in Adrianne Russell, "The Media Needs a History Lesson when Addressing Civic Unrest, Says the Director of the African American History Museum," Smithsonian.com, May 1, 2015. smithsonianmag.com/smithsonian-institution/media-needs-history-lesson-addressing-civic-unrest-director-african-american-history-museum-180955140/.

Former NFL player and black rights activist Wade Davis said of the NFL protests: "What Kaepernick did was disrupt one of our most treasured sports. Whether you agree with his tactics or not … the larger conversation is what he is protesting about."[72] Other NFL players also began protesting in this way, following Kaepernick's example.

A New Player in the Game: Social Media

Although the hashtag #BlackLivesMatter began on Facebook, it came to life on

In 2016, hundreds of Black Lives Matter protesters gathered in Times Square to protest police brutality that resulted in the deaths of several African American men.

Twitter and has since been tweeted more than 30 million times. In 2011, #Occupy-WallStreet brought millions of protesters on Twitter to the cause. In 2014, when the media reproduced a menacing portrait of black police brutality victim Michael Brown, #IfTheyGunnedMeDown proved just how scary or innocent the same user could look in two different photographs. In 2015 and 2016, #OscarsSoWhite evolved into major black celebrities boycotting the Academy Awards ceremony. In many ways, social media has reinvented activism, in particular how it is done and who participates in it.

Many social media platforms, such as Facebook, do not allow for quick masses to unify and spread a specific piece of content because users are only connected to their own relatively small community. However, a tweet can quickly be read and shared by millions, even by non-followers of an issue, which means that there exists today an incredibly small distance between the once-powerless and the very powerful.

The Slow Progress of Change

There will always be something to protest. Today, the number of subjects deserving organized action may seem overwhelming to some. Documentaries, news investigations, editorial articles, speeches at awards shows, and lyrics can expose issues, and social media platforms are now seen as playing a vital role in the activist dialogue as well. Social media can move people quickly to action, but it can be difficult to measure the change it brings about. How can shares, hashtags, retweets, or upvotes be measured? Can votes not cast be counted? People who would never describe themselves as activists are able to participate in protests online with little effort or fallout. However, these protests are also fragmented across many issues, and all vie for airtime in the 24-hour news cycle that soon wipes away each problem with the next one.

Some people thought that the civil rights leaders of the 1960s were asking for too much too fast. The same was said of abolitionists and suffragettes throughout their fights. This is not only a sentiment from people who have had the luxury of a life without racism, slavery, sexism, or lack of health care coverage. Sometimes, this is a legitimate concern by people who know that change is a difficult thing to push for and are anxious about the great, and sometimes violent, potential for resistance to change. Clearly, though, history is filled with plenty of people who felt their cause was worth the risk—even, at times, the risk of death. Change has shuffled slowly forward because of their unblinking tenacity to make it happen.

Notes

Introduction:
The Importance of
Protests and Riots

1. Ralph F. Young, *Dissent in America: The Voices That Shaped a Nation*. New York, NY: Pearson Education, 2006, p. xxi.
2. Martin Luther King Jr., "I've Been to the Mountaintop," American Rhetoric, updated February 7, 2017. www.americanrhetoric.com/speeches/mlkivebeentothemountaintop.htm.
3. Paul A. Gilje, *Rioting in America*. Bloomington, IN: Indiana University Press, 1996, p. 1.

Chapter One:
Same as It Ever Was

4. Quoted in Young, *Dissent in America*, p. xxii.
5. Quoted in Alan Hirsch and Tim Catchim, *The Permanent Revolution: Apostolic Imagination and Practice for the 21st Century Church*. San Francisco, CA: Wiley, 2012, "An Understanding That Many Want the Pioneer to Fail."
6. Henry David Thoreau, *On the Duty of Civil Disobedience*. Project Gutenberg, 2004. www.gutenberg.org/files/71/71-h/71-h.htm.
7. Quoted in Wai-chee Dimock,

Through Other Continents: American Literature Across Deep Time. Princeton, NJ: Princeton University Press, 2006, p. 20.
8. Quoted in Jack E. White, "Marching for a Dream," *TIME*, March 31, 2003. content.time.com/time/specials/packages/article/0,28804,1977881_1977891_1978393,00.html.
9. Quoted in Maggie Fox, "March for Science: Scientists Hit Streets to Demand Respect, Funding," NBC News, April 21, 2017. www.nbcnews.com/health/health-news/march-science-scientists-hit-streets-demand-respect-funding-n749486.
10. Young, *Dissent in America*, p. xxii.
11. Quoted in Charles V. Hamilton, *Urban Violence*. Chicago, IL: University of Chicago, 1969, p. 7.
12. Gilje, *Rioting in America*, p. 5.
13. Quoted in Daniel Polsby and David D. Haddock, "Understanding Riots," Learn Liberty, December 30, 2016. www.learnliberty.org/blog/why-riots-happen/.
14. Gilje, *Rioting in America*, p. 7.

Chapter Two:
Vocal Citizens

15. Quoted in Richard Colton, "Shays

Rebellion," National Park Service. www.nps.gov/spar/historyculture/shays-rebellion.htm.

16. "The Bill of Rights: A Transcription," National Archives, accessed December 7, 2017. www.archives.gov/founding-docs/bill-of-rights-transcript.

17. Quoted in Howard Zinn and Anthony Arnove, *Voices of a People's History of the United States*. New York, NY: Seven Stories, 2004, p. 81.

18. Page Smith, *A New Age Now Begins: A People's History of the American Revolution*, vol. 1. New York, NY: McGraw-Hill, 1976, p. 251.

19. Quoted in "The Bonus Army," EyeWitness to History, accessed December 8, 2017. www.eyewitnesstohistory.com.

20. Quoted in Albert Marrin, *FDR and the American Crisis*. New York, NY: Ember, 2016, p. 112.

21. Danika Worthington, "Meet the Disabled Activists from Denver who Changed a Nation," *Denver Post*, July 5, 2017. www.denverpost.com/2017/07/05/adapt-disabled-activists-denver/.

22. Worthington, "Meet the Disabled Activists from Denver who Changed a Nation."

23. Wilbert Rideau, "When Prisoners Protest," *New York Times*, July 16, 2013. www.nytimes.com/2013/07/17/opinion/when-prisoners-protest.html.

24. Heather Ann Thompson, "U.S. Prisoner Protest: Why Listening to the Voices of the Incarcerated Matters," *Newsweek*, October 25, 2016. www.newsweek.com/us-prison-protest-justice-reform-513580.

25. Quoted in J. Oliver Conroy, "The Long Tail of the Attica Prison Riot," *Morning News*, accessed December 8, 2017. themorningnews.org/article/the-long-tail-of-the-attica-prison-riot.

Chapter Three: Protesting War

26. "From John Adams to Hezekiah Niles, 13 February 1818," National Archives Founders Online, accessed December 8, 2017. founders.archives.gov/documents/Adams/99-02-02-6854.

27. Howard Zinn, "Opposing the War Party," HowardZinn.org, May 4, 2004, www.howardzinn.org/opposing-the-war-party/.

28. Quoted in Howard Zinn, *A People's History of the United States*. New York, NY: Perennial Classics, 2001, p. 370.

29. Quoted in Howard Zinn, *Postwar America, 1945–1971*. Cambridge, MA, 2002, p. 222.

30. Quoted in "Muhammad Ali—In His Own Words," BBC, June 4, 2016. www.bbc.com/sport/boxing/16146367.

31. Quoted in Bob Ostertag, *People's Movements, People's Press: The Journalism of Social Justice Movements*. Boston, MA: Beacon Press, 2006, p. 124.

32. Quoted in "The Kent State Shootings, 35 Years Later," NPR, May 4, 2005. www.npr.org/templates/story/story.php?storyId=4630596.

33. Quoted in Young, *Dissent in America*, p. 775.

34. Quoted in Burt Berlowe, *The Compassionate Rebel Revolution: Ordinary People Changing the World*. Minneapolis, MN: Mill City Press, 2011, p. 49.

35. Quoted in Associated Press, "Thousands Protest 6th Anniv. of Iraq War," CBS News, March 21, 2009. www.cbsnews.com/stories/2009/03/21/national/main4881873.shtml.

40. Gilje, *Rioting in America*, p. 145.

41. Quoted in Francis X. Donnelly, "UAW's Battles Shape History," *Detroit News*, September 16, 2008. detnews.com/article/20080916/AUTO01/809160319/0/AUTO01/UAW-s-battles-shapehistory.

42. "Cesar Chavez: In His Own Words," The Fight in the Fields, accessed December 12, 2017. www.fightinthefields.net/cesarchavez4.html.

43. Quoted in Ralph W. Conant, *The Prospects for Revolution: A Study of Riots, Civil Disobedience, and Insurrection in Contemporary America*. New York, NY: Harper and Row, 1971, p. 7.

Chapter Four:
Workers' Rights

36. "Obama Labor Day Speech at AFL-CIO Picnic: Full Video, Text," *Huffington Post*, last updated December 7, 2017. www.huffingtonpost.com/2009/09/07/obama-laborday-speech-at_n_278772.html.

37. Quoted in Zinn, *A People's History of the United States*, p. 223.

38. "The Great Strike, *Harper's Weekly*, August 11, 1877," ExplorePAHistory, accessed December 12, 2017. explorepahistory.com/odocument.php?docId=1-4-1CF.

39. Quoted in Priscilla Murolo and A.B. Chitty, *From the Folks Who Brought You the Weekend: A Short, Illustrated History of Labor in the United States*. New York, NY: The New Press, 2001, p. 151.

Chapter Five:
The Melting Pot

44. David Boesel and Peter H. Rossi, *Cities Under Siege: An Anatomy of the Ghetto Riots, 1964–1968*. New York, NY: Basic Books, 1971, p. 285.

45. "Lakota Accounts of the Massacre at Wounded Knee," PBS, accessed December 12, 2017. www.pbs.org/weta/thewest/resources/archives/eight/wklakota.htm.

46. Quoted in "Wounded Knee," *American Experience: We Shall Remain*, PBS, 2009. www.pbs.org/wgbh/amex/weshallremain/files/transcripts/WeShallRemain_5_transcript.pdf.

47. Quoted in *National Association for the Advancement of Colored People, Thirty Years of Lynching in the*

United States, 1889–1918. New York, NY: National Association for the Advancement of Colored People, 1919, p. 25.

48. Eric Foner, *Reconstruction: America's Unfinished Revolution, 1863–1877.* New York: Harper and Row, 1989, p. 537.

49. Allison Keyes, "The East St. Louis Race Riot Left Dozens Dead, Devastating a Community on the Rise," *Smithsonian,* June 30, 2017. smithsonianmag.com/smithsonian-institution/east-st-louis-race-riot-left-dozens-dead-devastating-community-on-the-rise-180963885/.

50. Chicago Commission on Race Relations, *The Negro in Chicago: A Study of Race Relations and a Race Riot.* Chicago, IL: University of Chicago Press, 1922, p. 598.

51. Rosa Parks and Gregory J. Reed, *Quiet Strength: The Faith, the Hope, and the Heart of a Woman Who Changed the Nation.* Grand Rapids, MI: Zondervan, 1994, p. 26.

52. James Meredith, *Three Years in Mississippi.* Bloomington, IN: Indiana University Press, 1966, p. 273.

53. Quoted in Herbert Aptheker, ed., *A Documentary History of the Negro People in the United States 1960–1968: From the Alabama Protests to the Death of Martin Luther King, Jr.,* vol. 7. New York, NY: Carol, 1994, p. 196.

54. Christopher Wilson, "Finding Lessons for Today's Protests in the History of Political Activism,"
Smithsonian, December 6, 2016. smithsonianmag.com/smithsonian-institution/finding-lessons-todays-protests-history-political-activism-180961309/.

55. Quoted in Nhien Nguyen, "Remembering Vincent Chin," *International Examiner,* June 19 to July 2, 2002.

Chapter Six:
A Struggle Throughout History

56. Quoted in Miriam Gurko, *The Ladies of Seneca Falls: The Birth of the Woman's Rights Movement.* New York, NY: MacMillan, 1974, p. 307.

57. Quoted in Mark Thompson, ed., *Long Road to Freedom: The Advocate History of the Gay and Lesbian Movement.* New York, NY: St. Martin's, 1994, p. 1.

58. Quoted in Lou Chibbaro Jr., "Gay Movement Boosted by '79 March on Washington," *Washington Blade,* November 5, 2004, www.washblade.com/2004/11-5/news/national/movement.cfm.

59. Laurel Thatcher Ulrich, *Well-Behaved Women Seldom Make History.* New York, NY: Knopf, 2007, p. xiii.

Epilogue:
History Repeating

60. Wade, *Urban Violence,* p. 10.

61. Quoted in Zinn and Arnove, *Voices of a People's History of the United States,* p. 69.

62. Quoted in Zinn and Arnove, *Voices of a People's History of the United States*, p. 208.
63. Quoted in William D. Griffin, *The Book of Irish Americans*. New York, NY: Random House, 1990, p. 146.
64. Quoted in "South Omaha Mob Wars on Greeks," *New York Times*, February 22, 1909, p. 1.
65. Quoted in Deborah Small, "Uprising: When Black America Launched a Violent Rebellion Against One of the Most Oppressive Societies on Earth," AlterNet, April 9, 2014. alternet.org/uprising-when-black-america-launched-violent-rebellion-against-one-most-oppressive-societies-earth.
66. Quoted in Small, "Uprising."
67. "CNN Presents: Race Rage, The Beating of Rodney King," CNN Presents, April 29, 2012. transcripts.cnn.com/TRANSCRIPTS/1204/29/cp.01.html.
68. Small, "Uprising."
69. Steph Solis, Molly Vorwerck, Jordan Friedman, and John Bacon, "'Justice for Trayvon' Rallies in 100 Cities Across USA," *USA Today*, July 20, 2013. www.usatoday.com/story/news/nation/2013/07/20/justice-trayvon-martin-vigils-zimmerman/2571025/.
70. John Eligon and Manny Fernandez, "In Protests From Midwest to Both Coasts, Fury Boils Over," *New York Times*, November 24, 2014. nytimes.com/2014/11/25/us/frustration-months-in-the-making-boils-over-on-the-streets-of-ferguson.html.
71. Monica Davey and Julie Bosman, "Protests Flare After Ferguson Police Officer Is Not Indicted," *New York Times*, November 24, 2014. nytimes.com/2014/11/25/us/ferguson-darren-wilson-shooting-michael-brown-grand-jury.html.
72. Quoted in John Branch, "The Awakening of Colin Kaepernick," *New York Times*, September 7, 2017. www.nytimes.com/2017/09/07/sports/colin-kaepernick-nfl-protests.html.

For More Information

Books

Bausum, Ann. *Stonewall: Breaking Out in the Fight for Gay Rights*. New York, NY: Viking, 2015.
This book covers the events leading up to and following the Stonewall riots and also describes the legacy the riots left behind.

Conkling, Winifred. *Votes for Women!: American Suffragists and the Battle for the Ballot*. Chapel Hill, NC: Algonquin Young Readers, 2018.
This book tells the personal and public stories of some of America's most well-known suffragettes and follows the movement from its earliest days in Seneca Falls, New York, to the passage of the 19th Amendment.

Edwards, Sue Bradford, and Duchess Harris. *Black Lives Matter*. Minneapolis, MN: Essential Library, 2016.
This book begins with the shootings that acted as a catalyst for the Black Lives Matter movement and details the work of activists within the movement to bring change to the U.S. legal system.

Engler, Mark, and Paul Engler. *This is an Uprising: How Nonviolent Revolt is Shaping the Twenty-First Century*. New York, NY: Nation Books, 2017.
This book details the recent history of the use of nonviolent protest to affect social and political change in America and around the world.

Rissman, Rebecca. *Rodney King and the L.A. Riots*. Minneapolis, MN: ABDO Publishing Company, 2014.
This book follows the story of Rodney King from his brutal assault by Los Angeles police officers to the riots and outrage that spread across the nation when the officers were found not guilty.

Websites

"Follow the Path of the Freedom Riders in this Interactive Map"
www.smithsonianmag.com/history/ follow-path-freedom-riders- interactive-map-180962313/
This map shows the journey that more than a dozen black and white college students made in 1961 to the South to protest segregation and show their frustration with continuing discrimination.

Map of White Supremacy Mob Violence
www.monroeworktoday.org/explore/
This website is dedicated to presenting the history of lynch mobs in America and features an in-depth map of instances where people were killed by mob violence. There are thousands of points listed on the map, with even more omitted until more rigorous research is completed.

National Organization for Women (NOW)
www.now.org
The National Organization for Women fights for women's rights, and its website offers a history of the organization and information on issues concerning women.

Prisoners' Rights
www.aclu.org/issues/prisoners-rights
The American Civil Liberty Union's page for its National Prison Project includes sections on the following current prisoners' rights issues they are concerned with: medical and mental health care; solitary confinement; cruel, inhumane, and degrading conditions; civil liberties; and women in prison.

Index

Picture Credits

Cover Lindsay Brice/Contributor/Michael Ochs Archives/Getty Images; pp. 4–5 Mario Tama/Staff/Getty Images News/Getty Images; p. 6 (top) Francis Miller/Contributor/The LIFE Picture Collection/Getty Images; p. 6 (bottom left and right) New York Daily News Archive/Contributor/New York Daily News/Getty Images; p. 7 (top) Noam Galai/Contributor/WireImage/Getty Images; p. 7 (bottom) Funcrunch/Wikimedia Commons; pp. 10, 11, 52, 58, 65 Bettmann/Contributor/Bettmann/Getty Images; p. 14 Universal History Archive/Contributor/Universal Images Group/Getty Images; p. 18 Scott Olson/Staff/Getty Images News/Getty Images; p. 19 Daryl L/Shutterstock.com; p. 22 Underwood Archives/Contributor/Archives Photos/Getty Images; p. 23 (top left) rook76/Shutterstock.com; p. 23 (top middle, top right, bottom middle) catwalker/Shutterstock.com; p. 23 (bottom left) EtiAmmos/Shutterstock.com; p. 23 (bottom right) chrisdorney/Shutterstock.com; p. 27 North Wind Picture Archives; p. 28 Anonymous/Getty Images; p. 30 Historical/Contributor/Corbis Historical/Getty Images; pp. 33, 46–47 MANDEL NGAN/Staff/AFP/Getty Images; p. 34 Keystone/Stringer/Hulton Archive/Getty Images; pp. 38–39 Hulton Archive/Stringer/Archive Photos/Getty Images; pp. 40–41 Lee Lockwood Contributor/The LIFE Images Collection/Getty Images; pp. 42–43 Howard Ruffner/Contributor/Archive Photos/Getty Images; p. 45 The Washington Post/Contributor/The Washington Post/Getty Images; pp. 53, 54 Arthur Schatz/Contributor/The LIFE Picture Collection/Getty Images; p. 61 Ralph Crane/Contributor/The LIFE Picture Collection/Getty Images; p. 64 UniversalImagesGroup/Contributor/Universal Images Group/Getty Images; p. 69 Bob Daemmrich/Alamy Stock Photo; p. 72 Courtesy of the Library of Congress; p. 74 Bill Pugliano/Stringer/Getty Images News/Getty Images; p. 75 mark peterson/Contributor/Corbis Historical/Getty Images; p. 77 AP Photo; p. 79 Max Whittaker/Stringer/Getty Images News/Getty Images; p. 80 KENA BETANCUR/Stringer/AFP/Getty Images; p. 85 okili77/Shutterstock.com; p. 86 MIKE NELSON/Staff/AFP/Getty Images; p. 88 Michael Zagaris/Contributor/Getty Images Sport/Getty Images; p. 90 Pacific Press/Contributor/LightRocket/Getty Images.

About the Author

Historian **Joan Stoltman** is the author of more than 70 kindergarten through 5th-grade educational books, as well as several 6th-grade through 12th-grade history books. Because of her art and architecture history degrees, she has a unique method of research, often going "straight to the source" (artists, designers, craftspeople, and architects) to learn how people in history felt. Having been raised by a social psychology professor dad, she is versed in advertising and consumer activist history. Her mother's influence, on the other hand, influences how she spends most of her time: with her dog, at her local library, crafting, working with children, and volunteering.